The Unofficial Schitt's Creek Drink Cookbook

55+ Amazing & Easy Drinks Recipes Inspired by Schitt's Creek

Jeanette Slater

© Copyright 2021 - All rights reserved.

The content contained within this book may not be reproduced, duplicated or transmitted without direct written permission from the author or the publisher.

Under no circumstances will any blame or legal responsibility be held against the publisher, or author, for any damages, reparation, or monetary loss due to the information contained within this book, either directly or indirectly.

Legal Notice:

This book is copyright protected. It is only for personal use. You cannot amend, distribute, sell, use, quote or paraphrase any part, or the content within this book, without the consent of the author or publisher.

Disclaimer Notice:

Please note the information contained within this document is for educational and entertainment purposes only. All effort has been executed to present accurate, up to date, reliable, complete information. No warranties of any kind are declared or implied. Readers acknowledge that the author is not engaged in the rendering of legal, financial, medical or professional advice. The content within this book has been derived from various sources. Please consult a licensed professional before attempting any techniques outlined in this book.

By reading this document, the reader agrees that under no circumstances is the author responsible for any losses, direct or indirect, that are incurred as a result of the use of the information contained within this document, including, but not limited to, errors, omissions, or inaccuracies.

Table of Contents

Introduction

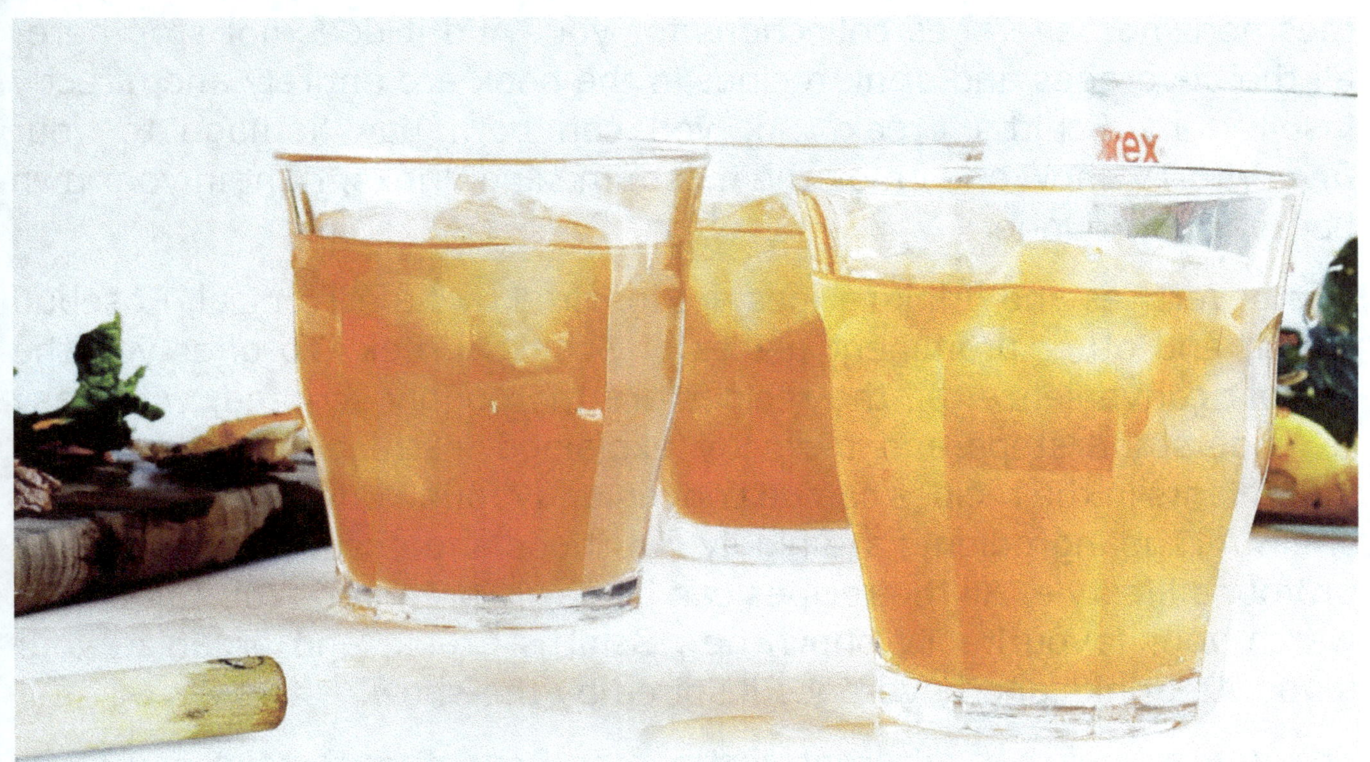

Life in the present world has grown to be so much workaholic and stressed out and has become one of the prominent reasons for leading anxiety and depression rates globally. Comedy can become a game-changer in making the world less-depressive and merrier by offering relief from the hectic daily routine. Comedy provides you with the charm to understand the beautiful and peaceful side of life. Blending food and comedy together is by far the most appealing remedy to let you forget the harshness life throws at you and instead enjoy two of the most prominent blessings of life together.

We have worked really hard to give this idea an authentic touch and devised a cookbook known as the **"The Unofficial Schitt's Creek Drink Cookbook"**. It is basically originated from the infamous TV comedy show known as Schitt's Creek. The book is primarily inspired by Schitt's Creeks' characters and various prominent aspects of Emlade County. This particular cookbook inspired by Schitt's Creek. Focuses solely on drinks and beverages only. Moreover, it is irrelevant whether you are a home-cooked food lover or a regular dine-in fan at restaurants, bars, or cafés, the book, has one of the most amazing, delicious, and mesmerizing beverages collections for you. And it does not stop here; all the beverages and drink recipes in the book are entirely and directly inspired by Schitt's Creek. So, you can both pay homage to your favourite TV show and enjoy the most amazing drinks, right in your own backyard or lounge.

The beverages and drink recipes are inspired by Café Tropical, Rosebud Motel, and other prominent places of Schitt's Creek. To offer you the utmost convenience, all the recipes are thoroughly scripted, with easy to understand steps and perfectly explained instructions, and all the ingredients in the recipes can be conveniently found on any supermarket shelf. All the ingredients are highly nutritious and ensure a healthy and profound lifestyle. All the recipes can be easily prepared. You can binge-watch your favourite TV show, i.e., Schitt's Creek, and organize your favourite drinks and beverages inspired by the show.

The entire book has different sections and chapters to take you step-wise throughout the book and mesmerize you with the joy Schitt's Creek has to offer you in the real world. Moreover, every forthcoming chapter will bring new ingredients and newer recipes, making it seem exciting and catchy for you to remain to indulge in the magical and happy world of Schitt's Creek. The worth mentioning beverages and drinks recipes include Herb Ertlinger's Wine Spritzer and Twyla's Meadow Harvest Smoothie.

You don't have to panic about the difficulty level of the recipes, as the cookbook offers recipes for every expertise in cooking. However, all the recipes are provided with easily understandable instructions, so if you follow them profoundly, you will certainly not have any issue mastering the cookbook in a single go. Thus, **The Unofficial Schitt's Creek Drink Cookbook** gives you the opportunity to relive your favourite TV show, i.e., Schitt's Creek, and blend humour with food, to have one of the best feelings ever, and temporarily forget about all your worries.

Detox Drinks Recipes

Johnny Rose Ginger Orange Detox Juice

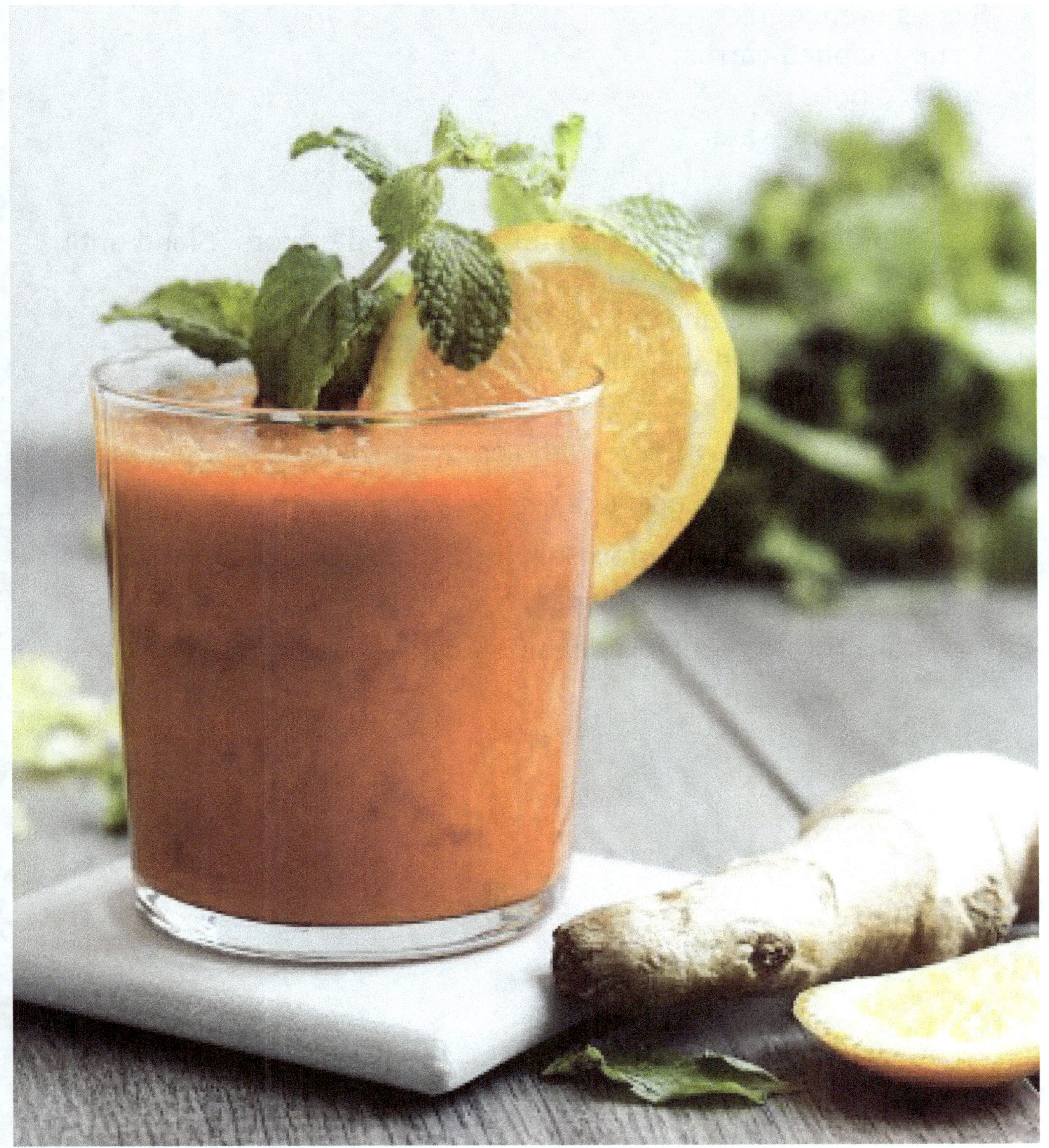

Preparation Time: 20 minutes
Servings: 4

Ingredients:

- 8 cups orange juice
- 1 cup chopped carrots
- 2 inch ginger
- 1 cup coconut water

Preparation:

1. In a blender, add ginger, coconut water, and carrots. Blend until smooth.
2. Strain the mixture and set aside.
3. Add orange juice in the mixture and pour it in serving glasses.
4. Serve and enjoy!

Serving Suggestions: Serve with some mint leaves on the top.

Variation Tip: You can also use fresh water instead of coconut water.

Nutritional Information per Serving:

Calories: 250| **Fat:** 1.2g| **Sat Fat:** 0.3g| **Carbohydrates:** 57.2g| **Fiber:** 2.5g| **Sugar:** 44.6g| **Protein:** 4.1g

Moira Rose Pomegranate Lemon Detox Water

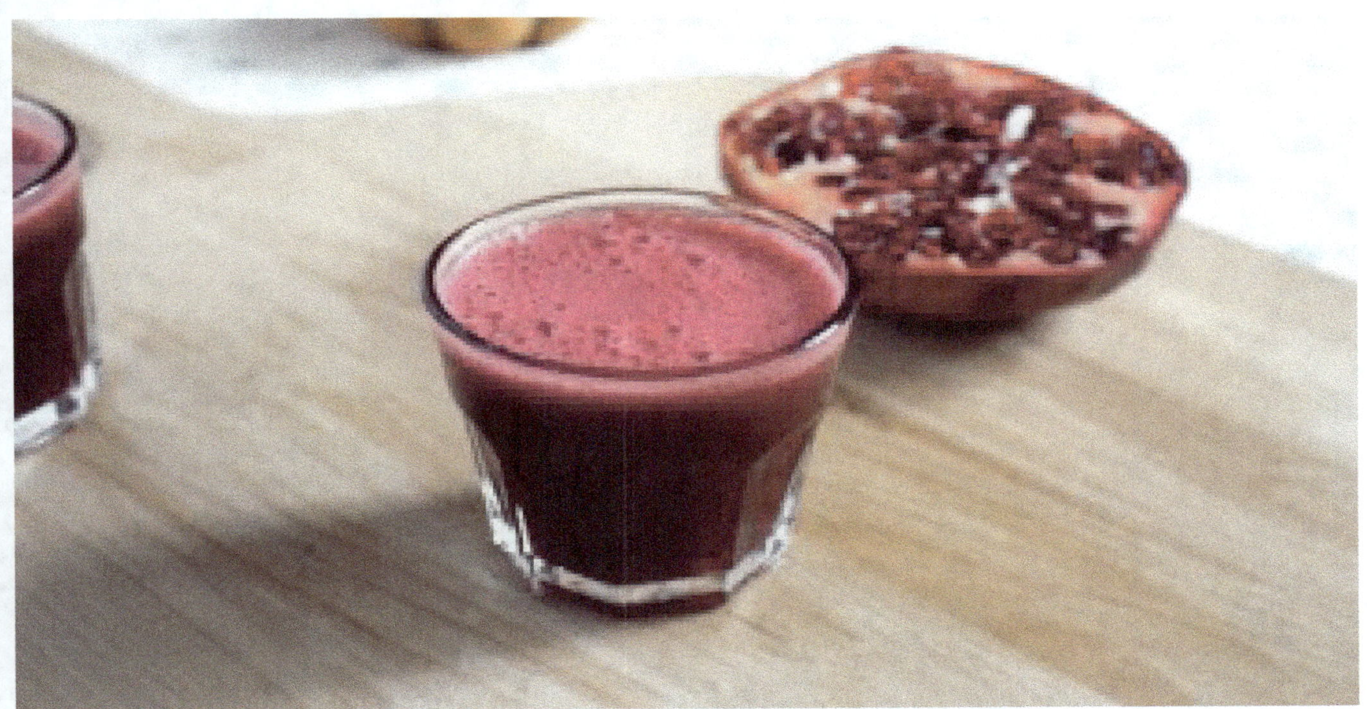

Preparation Time: 10 minutes
Servings: 4

Ingredients:

- 2 pomegranates, deseeded
- 2 lemons
- 4 cups water
- 2 slices of ginger

Preparation:

1. Add one cup water, pomegranates, lemons, and ginger in a blender and blend until a smooth mixture is formed.
2. Strain the mixture in a jug and add remaining one cup of water.
3. Pour in serving glasses and serve.

Serving Suggestions: Add ice in the glasses before serving.

Variation Tip: You can add cinnamon to enhance taste.

Nutritional Information per Serving:

Calories: 62| **Fat:** 0.1g| **Sat Fat:** 0g| **Carbohydrates:** 16.3g| **Fiber:** 1.4g| **Sugar:** 11.3g| **Protein:** 0.9g

David Rose Cinnamon Apple Cider Vinegar Detox

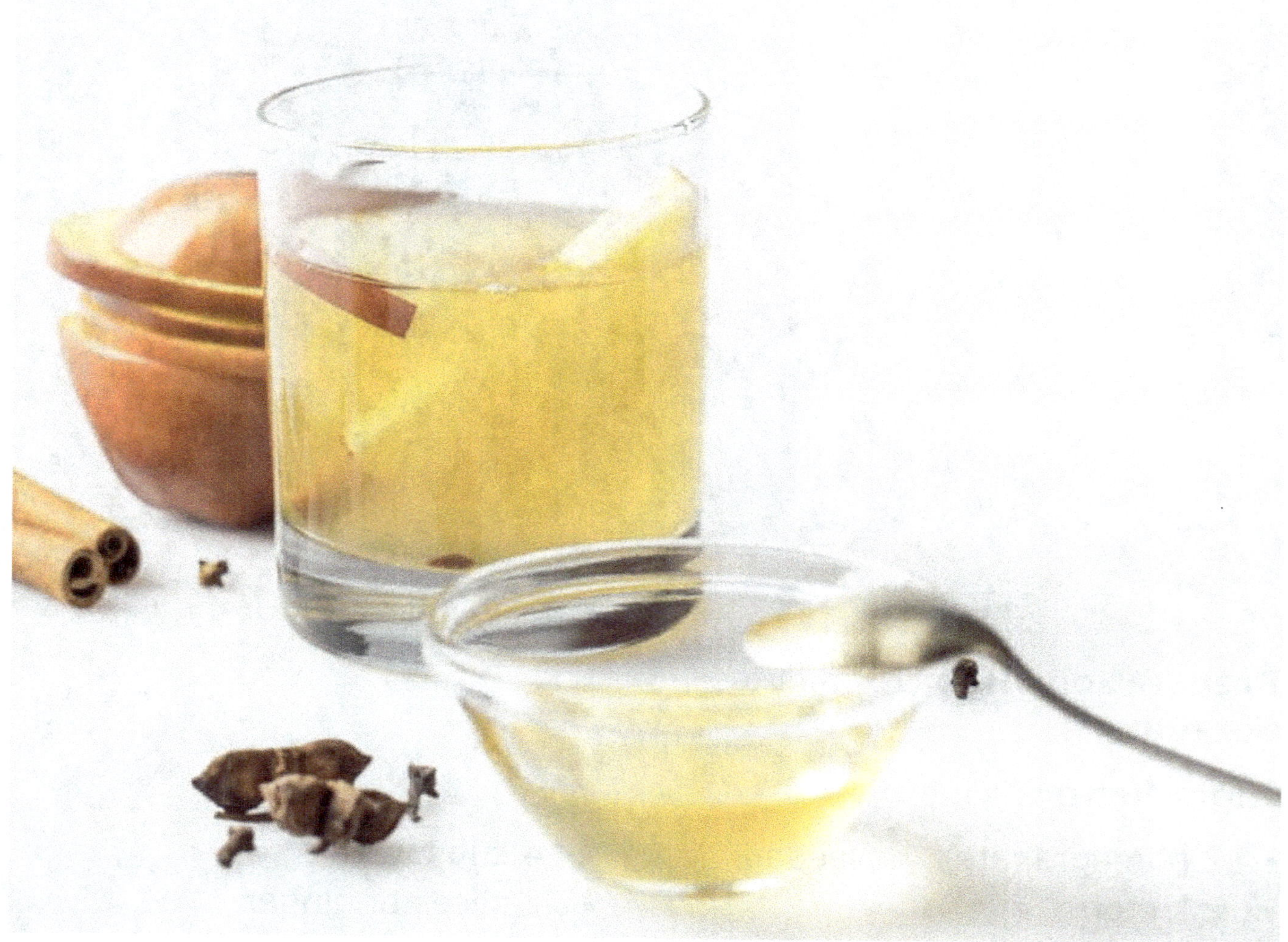

Preparation Time: 5 minutes
Servings: 1

Ingredients:

- 1 cup water
- 1 tablespoon apple cider vinegar
- ½ honey crisp apple
- ½ teaspoon cinnamon

Preparation:

1. Add water, apple cider vinegar, apple, and cinnamon in a blender.
2. Blend well to from a smooth mixture.

3. Take out and refrigerate.
4. Serve and enjoy!

Serving Suggestions: Serve with the topping of cinnamon stick and honey.

Variation Tip: Use vanilla extract to enhance taste.

Nutritional Information per Serving:

Calories: 33| **Fat:** 0.1g| **Sat Fat:** 0g| **Carbohydrates:** 8.4g| **Fiber:** 1.9g| **Sugar:** 5.6g| **Protein:** 0.2g

Alexis Rose Detox Ginger Lemonade

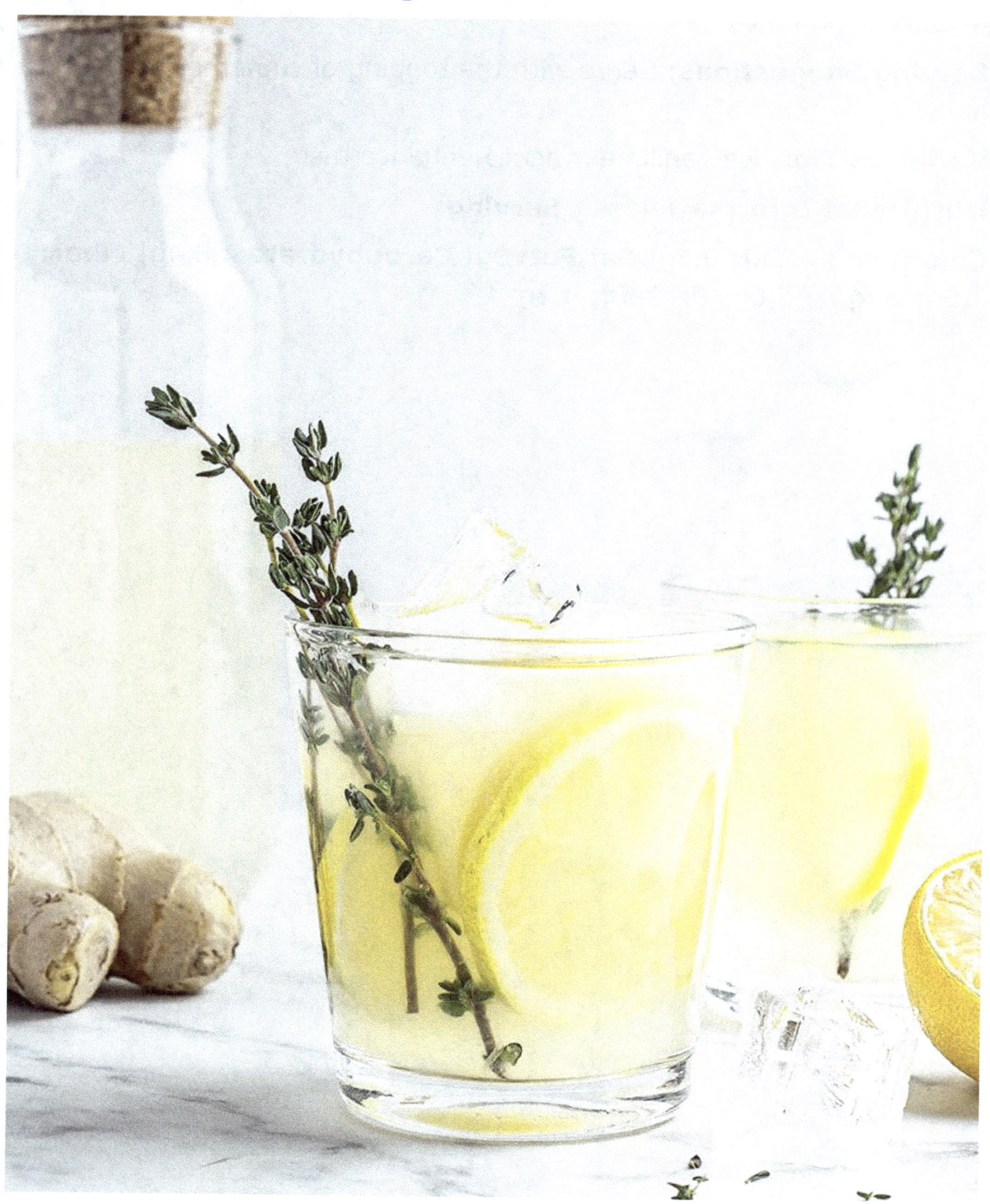

Preparation Time: 5 minutes
Servings: 1

Ingredients:

- 1 cup water
- 1 teaspoon lemon juice
- ½ inch ginger, sliced
- 1 teaspoon raw honey
- 2 tablespoons unfiltered apple cider vinegar

Preparation:

1. Add water and ginger in a blender. Blend well.
2. Then add honey, lemon juice, and apple cider vinegar.
3. Blend and pour in the glasses.
4. Serve and enjoy!

Serving Suggestions: Top with mint leaves and crushed ice before serving.

Variation Tip: You can also use coconut water.

Nutritional Information per Serving:

Calories: 40| **Fat:** 0.1g| **Sat Fat:** 0.1g| **Carbohydrates:** 10.5g| **Fiber:** 0.1g| **Sugar:** 5.9g| **Protein:** 0.1g

Jocelyn Schitt Mint Cucumber Lemon Detox

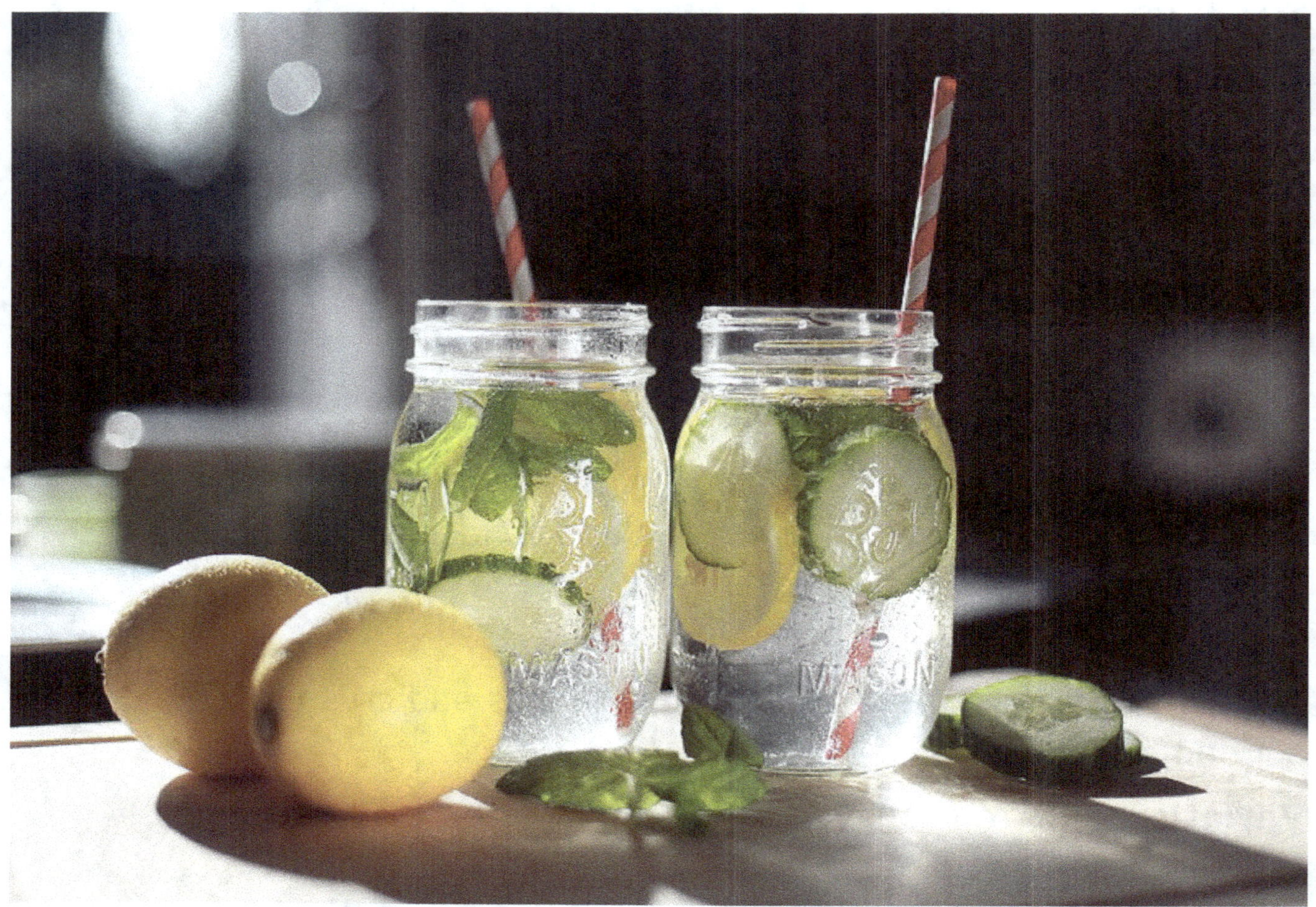

Preparation Time: 5 minutes

Servings: 4

Ingredients:

- 3 cups water
- 2 lemons
- 4 sprigs mint
- ½ cucumber, sliced

Preparation:

1. Add water in a jug.
2. Now, add juice from one lemon and let the mixture set for a while.

3. Now, add in cucumber slices, mint leaves, and lemon slices in the jug.
4. Let the mixture set for 2 to 3 hours and pour in serving glasses.
5. Serve and enjoy!

Serving Suggestions: Serve with crushed ice on the top.

Variation Tip: You can use more lemon to enhance taste.

Nutritional Information per Serving:

Calories: 19| **Fat:** 0.2g| **Sat Fat:** 0g| **Carbohydrates:** 5g| **Fiber:** 1.8g| **Sugar:** 1.4g| **Protein:** 0.9g

Mutt Schitt Sweet Apple Cider Vinegar Detox

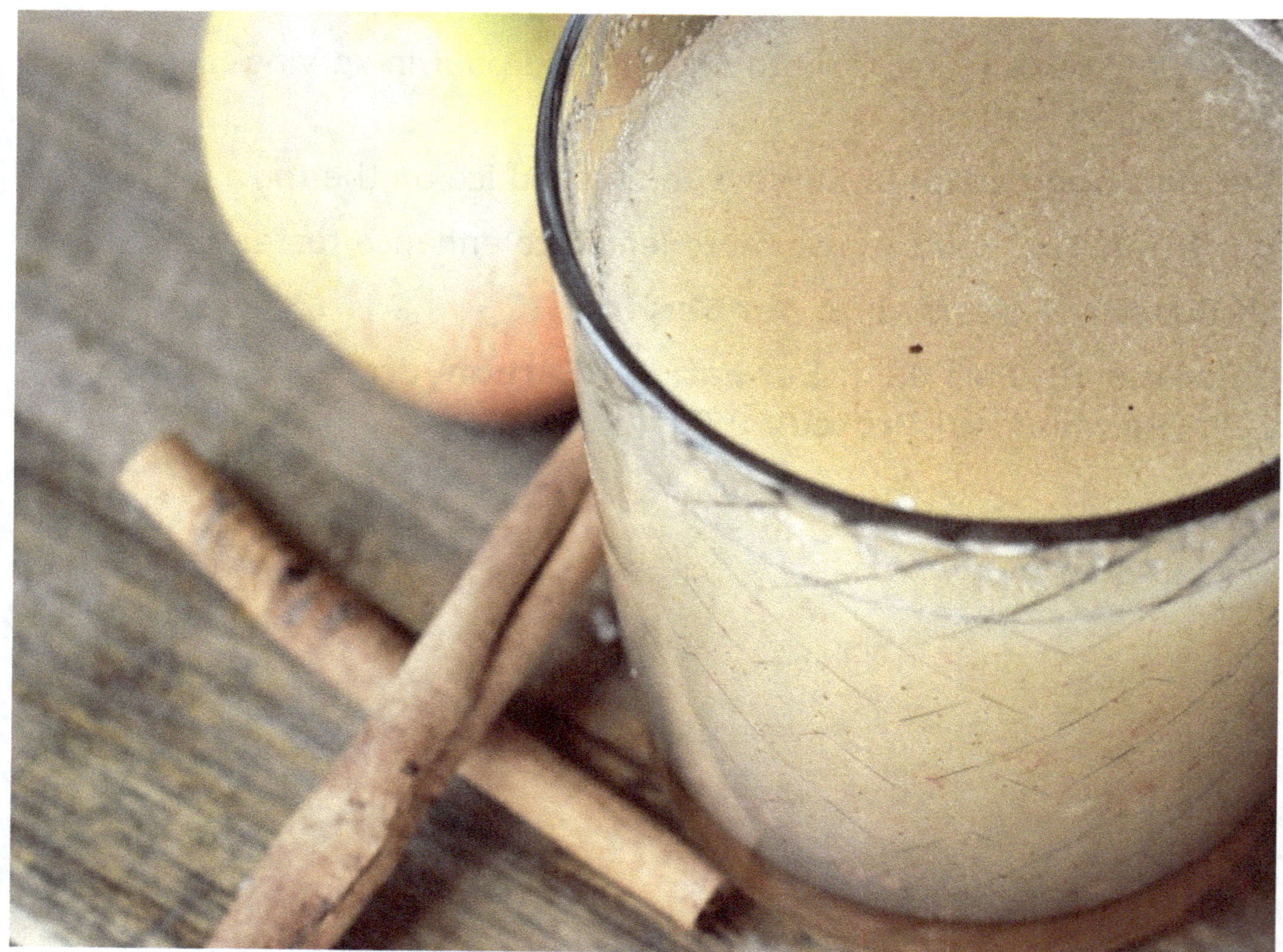

Preparation Time: 10 minutes
Servings: 2

Ingredients:

- 2 cups water
- 2 teaspoons maple syrup
- 2 tablespoons apple cider vinegar
- 1 teaspoon honey

Preparation:

1. Add apple cider vinegar, maple syrup, water, and honey in a blender.

2. Blend until a smooth mixture is formed.
3. Take out and top with ice.
4. Serve and enjoy!

Serving Suggestions: Serve with cinnamon powder on the top.

Variation Tip: You can omit honey if you want.

Nutritional Information per Serving:

Calories: 31| **Fat:** 0g| **Sat Fat:** 0g| **Carbohydrates:** 7.5g| **Fiber:** 0g| **Sugar:** 6.9g| **Protein:** 0g

Stevie Budd Fruit Infused Detox Water

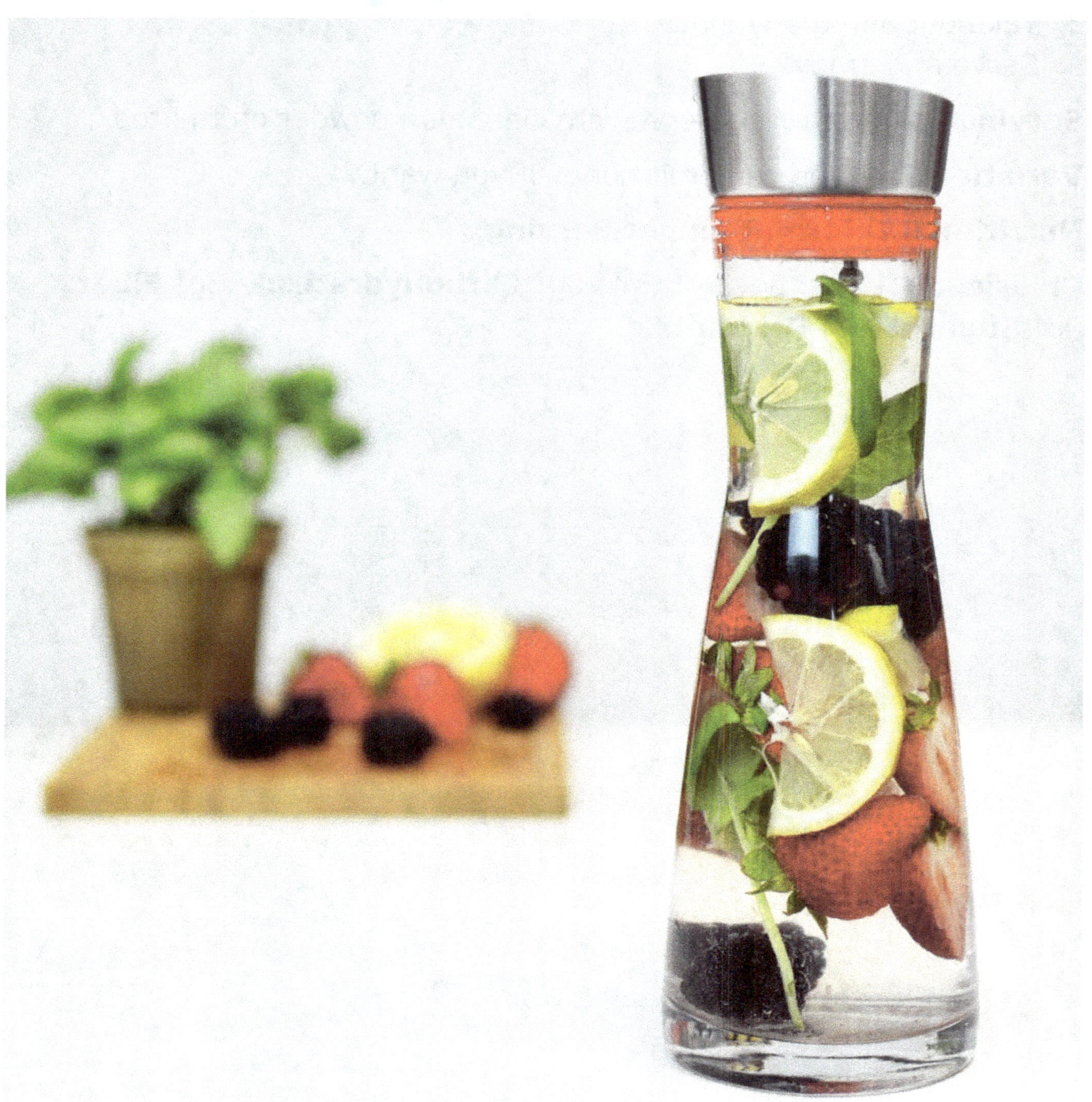

Preparation Time: 5 minutes
Servings: 2

Ingredients:

- 2 cups water

- ½ cup blackberries
- ½ cup strawberries
- 3 tablespoons lemon juice

Preparation:

1. Add water, and lemon juice in a jug. Mix well.
2. Now, add strawberries and blackberries in the jug and refrigerate for about 3 to 4 hours.
3. Take out and top with mint leaves.
4. Serve and enjoy!

Serving Suggestions: You can serve with the lemon slices on the top.

Variation Tip: You can also use blueberries or raspberries.

Nutritional Information per Serving:

Calories: 32| **Fat:** 0.5g| **Sat Fat:** 0.2g| **Carbohydrates:** 6.7g|

Fiber: 2.7g| **Sugar:** 4g| **Protein:** 0.9g

Roland Schitt Lemon Cayenne Pepper Detox

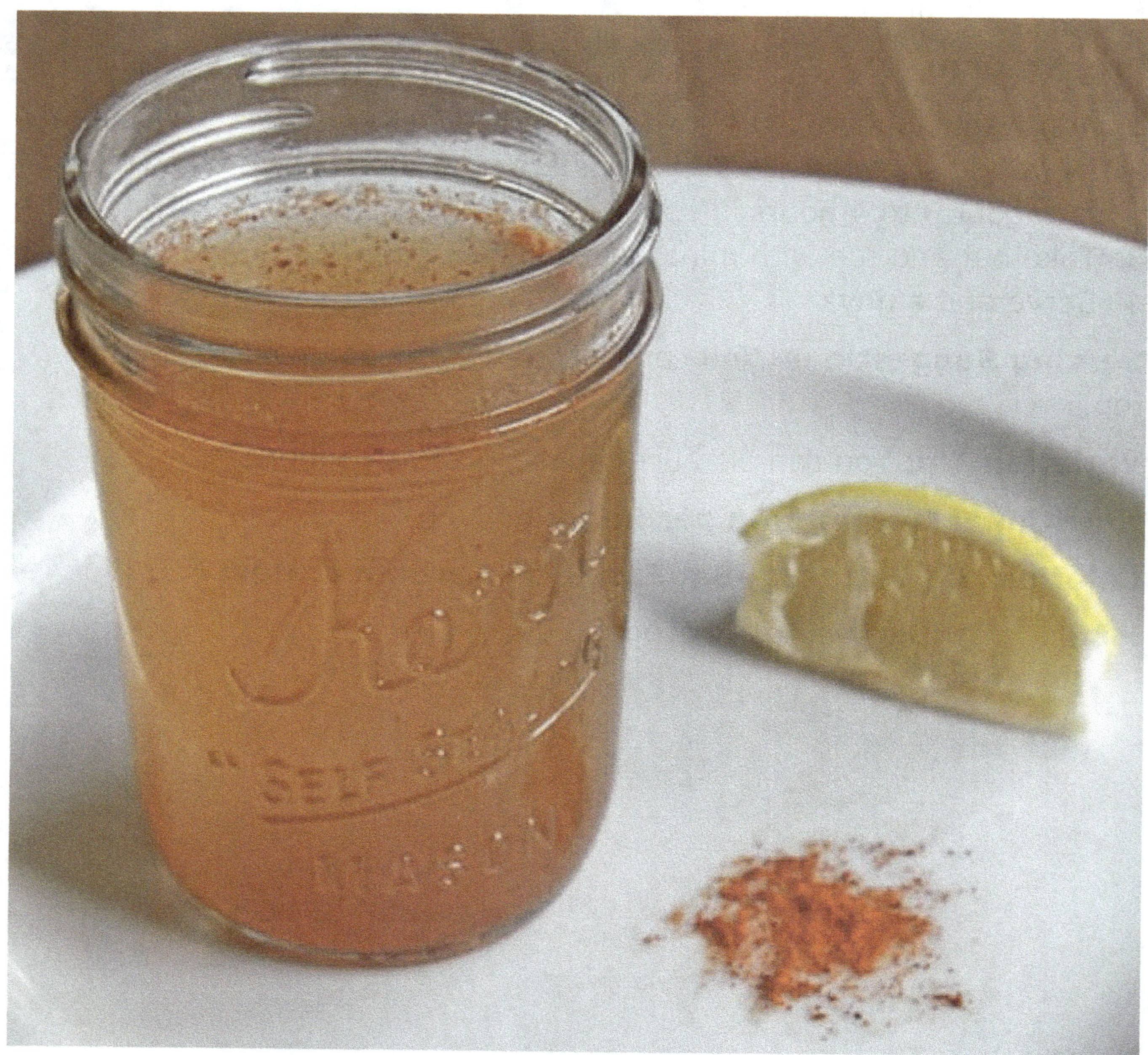

Preparation Time: 10 minutes
Servings: 2

Ingredients:

- 2 cups water
- ½ teaspoon cayenne pepper

- 2 tablespoons apple cider vinegar
- 2 tablespoons maple syrup
- 4 tablespoons lemon juice

Preparation:

1. Add water, cayenne pepper, maple syrup, apple cider vinegar, and lemon juice in a mixer.
2. Mix well and take out.
3. Add ice and serve.

Serving Suggestions: Serve with cinnamon on the top.

Variation Tip: You can add ginger to enhance taste.

Nutritional Information per Serving:

Calories: 64| **Fat:** 0.4g| **Sat Fat:** 0.3g| **Carbohydrates:** 14.5g|

Fiber: 0.2g| **Sugar:** 12.7g| **Protein:** 0.3g

Smoothie Recipes

Twyla Sands Mango Spinach Banana Smoothie

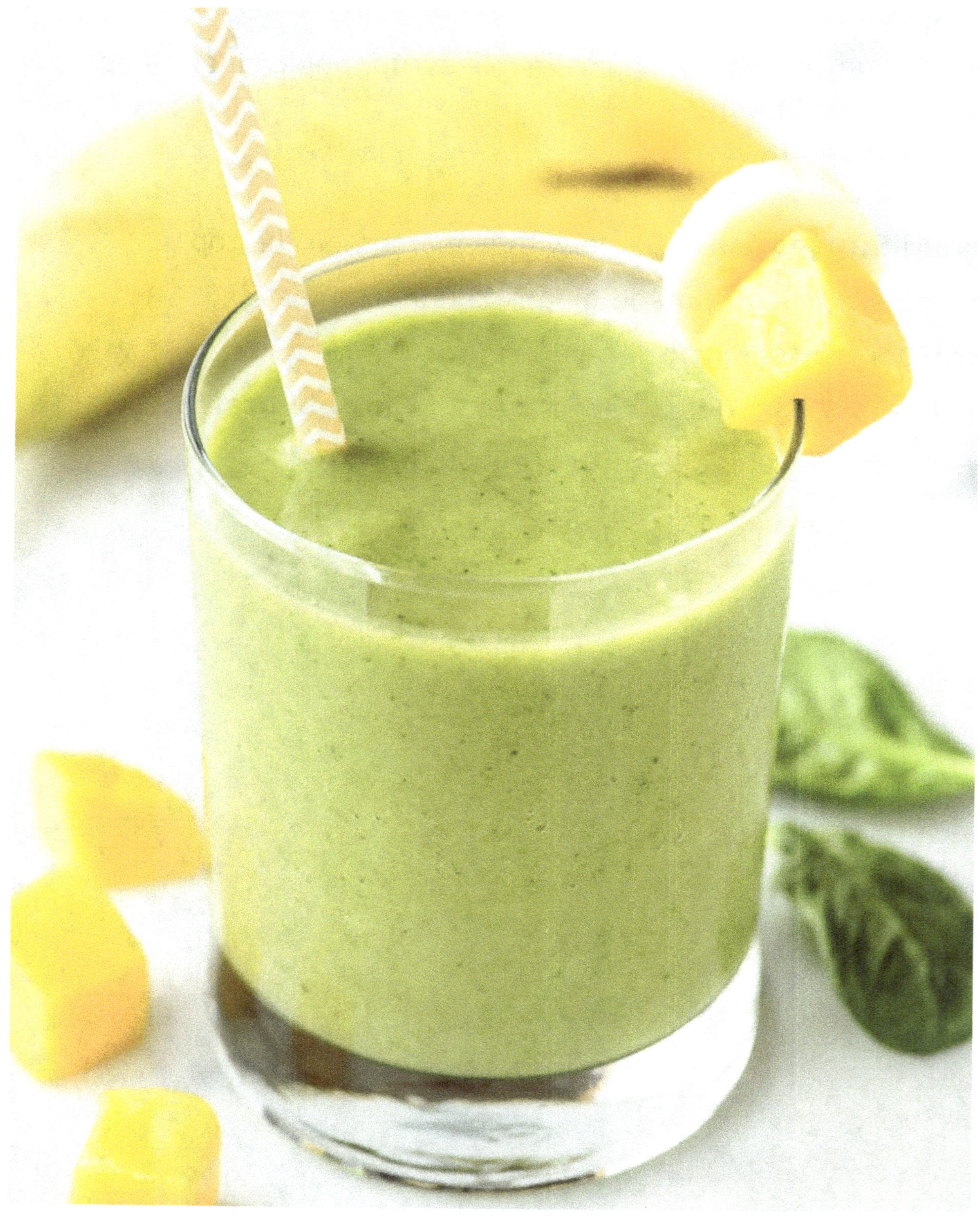

Preparation Time: 10 minutes
Servings: 2

Ingredients:

- 2 bananas, sliced
- 2 cups unsweetened almond milk
- 3 cups chopped baby spinach
- ½ cup water
- 1 cup chopped mango
- 1 scoop vanilla protein powder

Preparation:

1. Add bananas, mangoes, spinach, and almond milk in a blender. Blend well.
2. Now, add water and protein powder in the blender.
3. Blend until a smooth mixture is formed.
4. Take out and add ice in the smoothie.
5. Serve and enjoy!

Serving Suggestions: Top it with mint leaves.

Variation Tip: Coconut milk can also be used.

Nutritional Information per Serving:

Calories: 255| **Fat:** 4.6g| **Sat Fat:** 0.5g| **Carbohydrates:** 43.9g|

Fiber: 6.4g| **Sugar:** 26.4g| **Protein:** 15.8g

Robert Currie Coffee Banana Smoothie

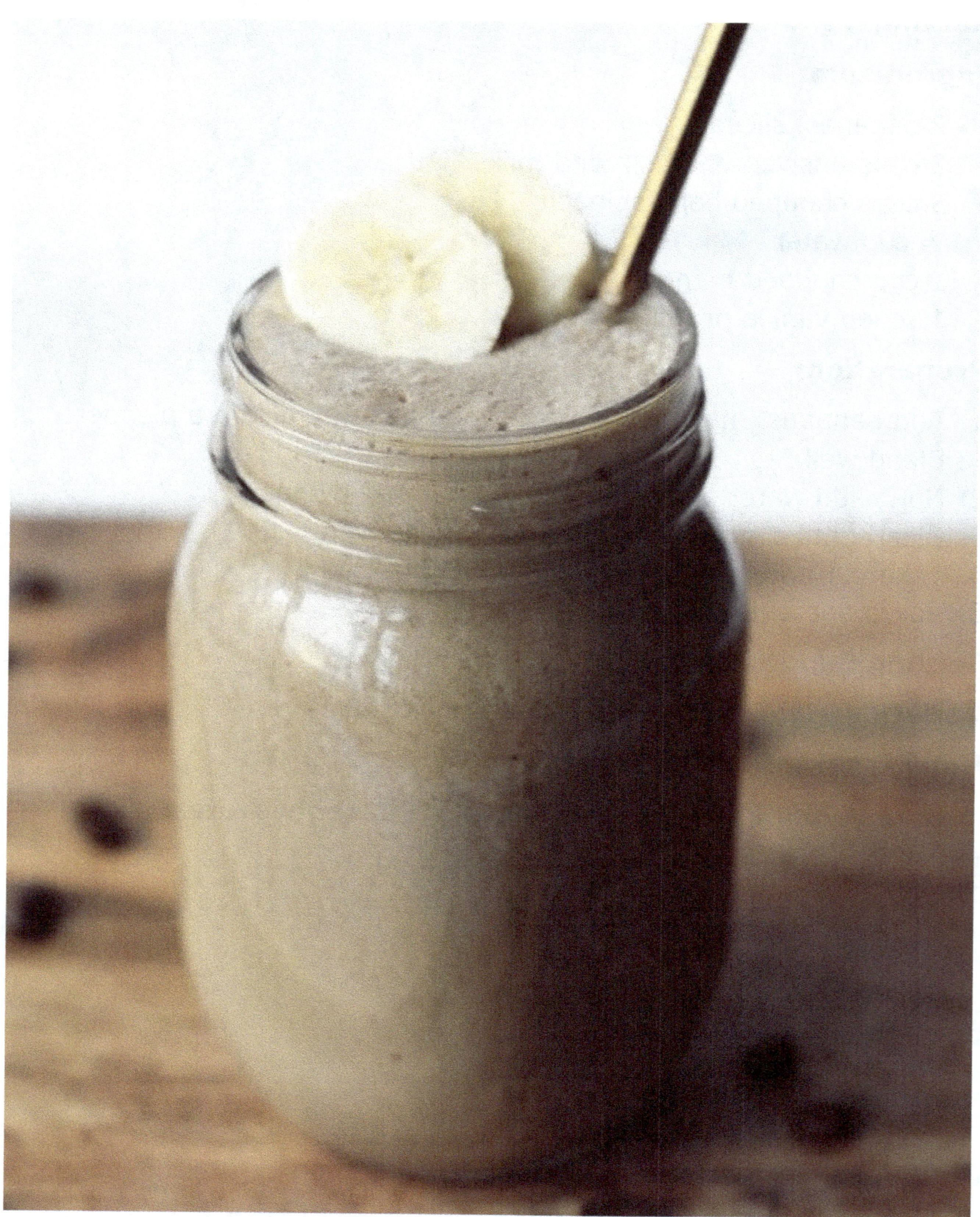

Preparation Time: 10 minutes
Servings: 2

Ingredients:

- 2 bananas
- 2 tablespoons unsweetened cocoa powder
- 2 cups strong brewed coffee
- 1 cup plain Greek yogurt
- 2 tablespoons honey

Preparation:

1. Add bananas, cocoa powder, coffee, yogurt, and honey in a food processor.
2. Pulse until a smooth mixture is formed.
3. Pour in the serving glasses and refrigerate for about one or two hours.
4. Serve and enjoy!

Serving Suggestions: Top with banana slices before serving.

Variation Tip: You can also add chocolate syrup to enhance taste.

Nutritional Information per Serving:

Calories: 261| **Fat:** 2.6g| **Sat Fat:** 1.6g| **Carbohydrates:** 51.7g|

Fiber: 4.9g| **Sugar:** 35.3g| **Protein:** 14.2g

Veronica Lee Peanut Butter Chocolate Smoothie

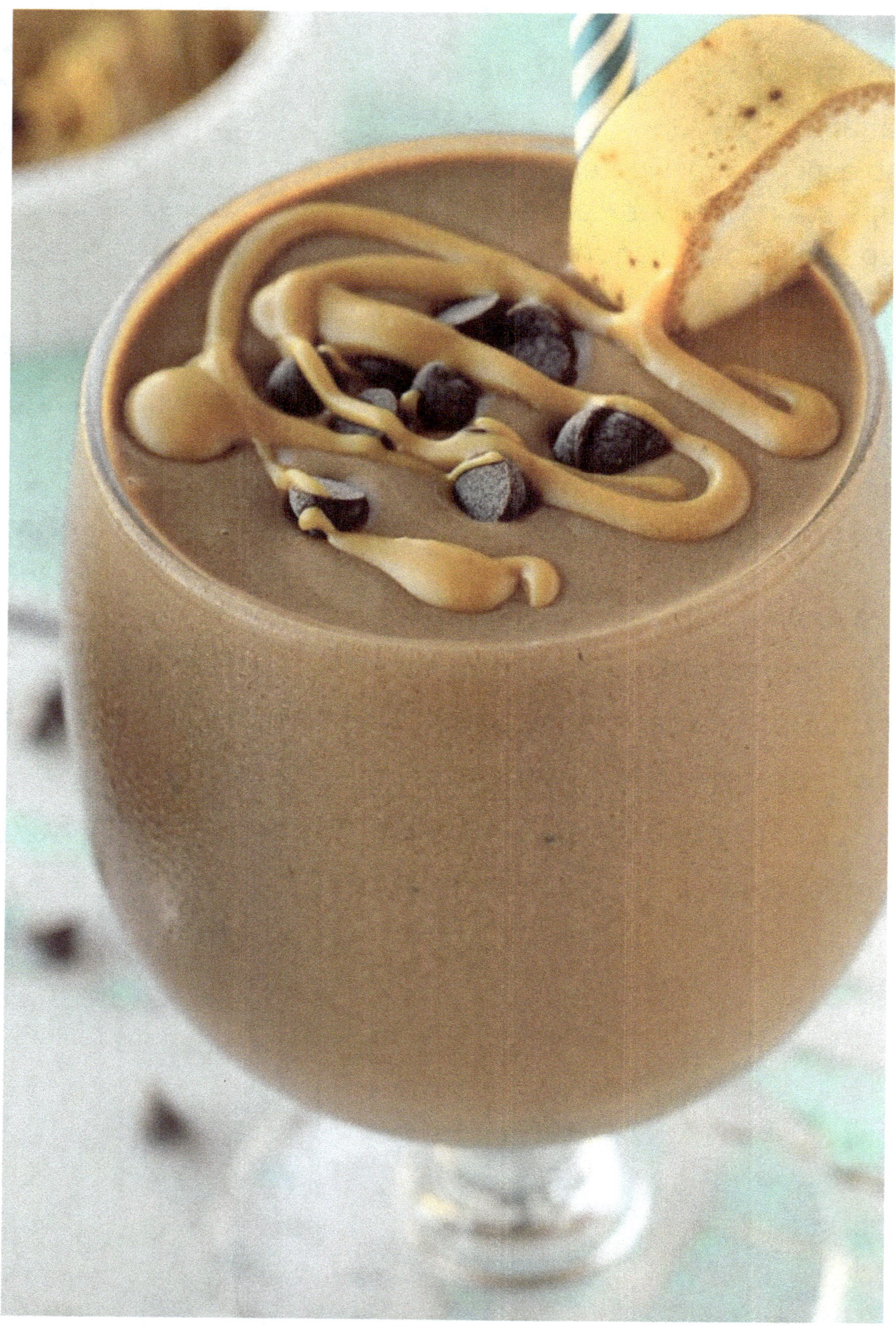

Preparation Time: 10 minutes

Servings: 4

Ingredients:

- 4 cups unsweetened coconut milk
- 4 tablespoons peanut butter
- 4 teaspoons unsweetened cocoa powder
- 2 tablespoons chocolate syrup
- 2 tablespoons chocolate chips

Preparation:

1. Add coconut milk, cocoa powder, chocolate syrup and peanut butter in a blender.
2. Blend until a smooth mixture is formed.
3. Take out and top with chocolate chips.
4. Serve and enjoy!

Serving Suggestions: Top with maple syrup before serving.

Variation Tip: You can also use almond milk.

Nutritional Information per Serving:

Calories: 704| **Fat:** 67.2g| **Sat Fat:** 53.7g| **Carbohydrates:** 26.7g|

Fiber: 7.3g| **Sugar:** 16.9g| **Protein:** 10.5g

Theodore Mullens Orange Smoothie

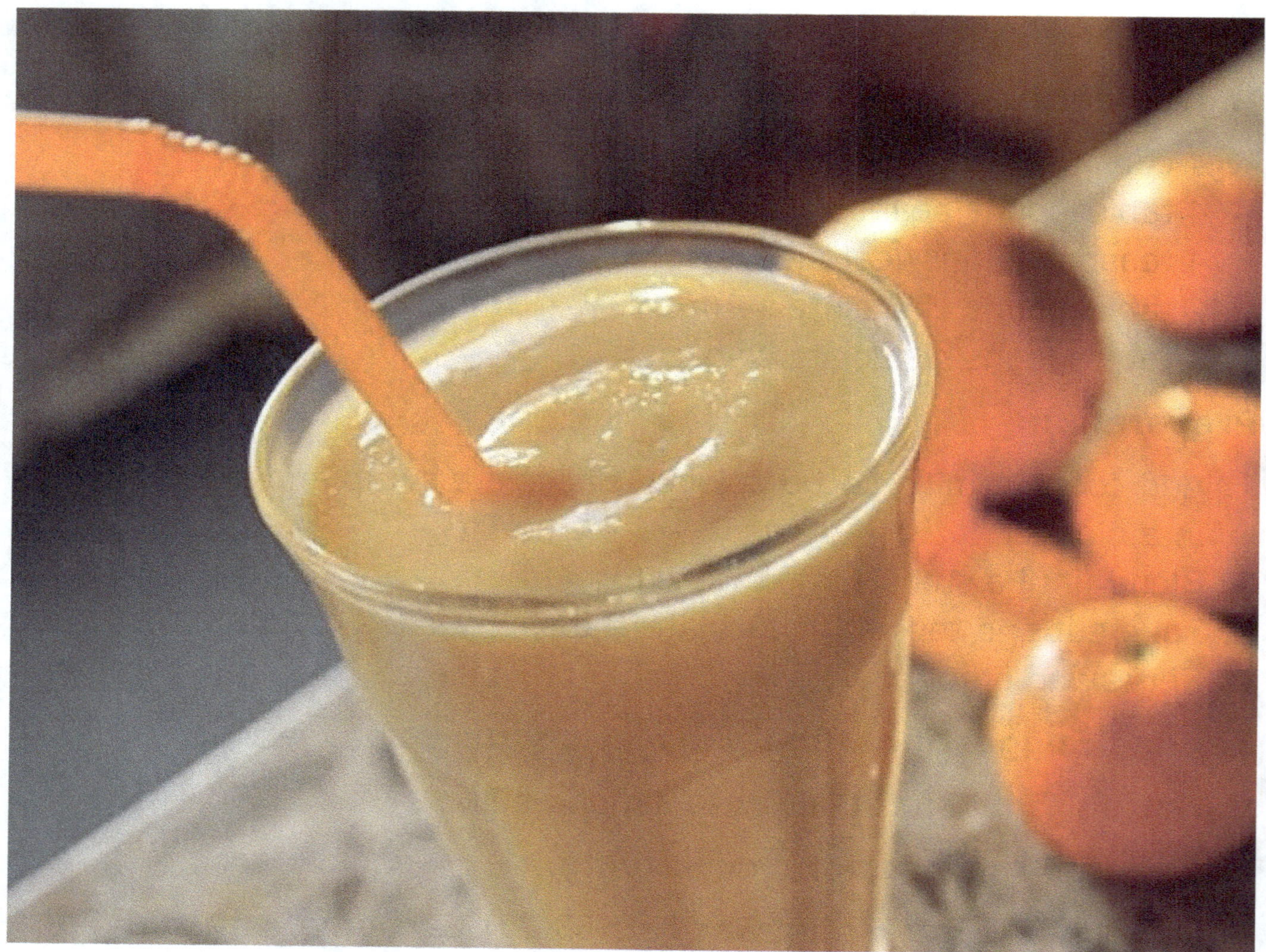

Preparation Time: 10 minutes
Servings: 4

Ingredients:

- 4 oranges, peeled
- 2 teaspoons vanilla extract
- 2 cups plain Greek yogurt
- 2 cups unsweetened soy milk
- 2 teaspoons maple syrup

Preparation:

1. Add oranges, vanilla extract, soy milk, and Greek yogurt in a food processor.
2. Pulse until a firm mixture is formed.
3. Pour the mixture in serving glasses and add maple syrup in it.
4. Serve and enjoy!

Serving Suggestions: Top with mint leaves before serving.

Variation Tip: You can use nut milk instead of soy milk.

Nutritional Information per Serving:

Calories: 247| **Fat:** 3.9g| **Sat Fat:** 1.3g| **Carbohydrates:** 36.3g|

Fiber: 5.2g| **Sugar:** 27.8g| **Protein:** 17.2g

Patrick Brewer Banana Strawberry Smoothie

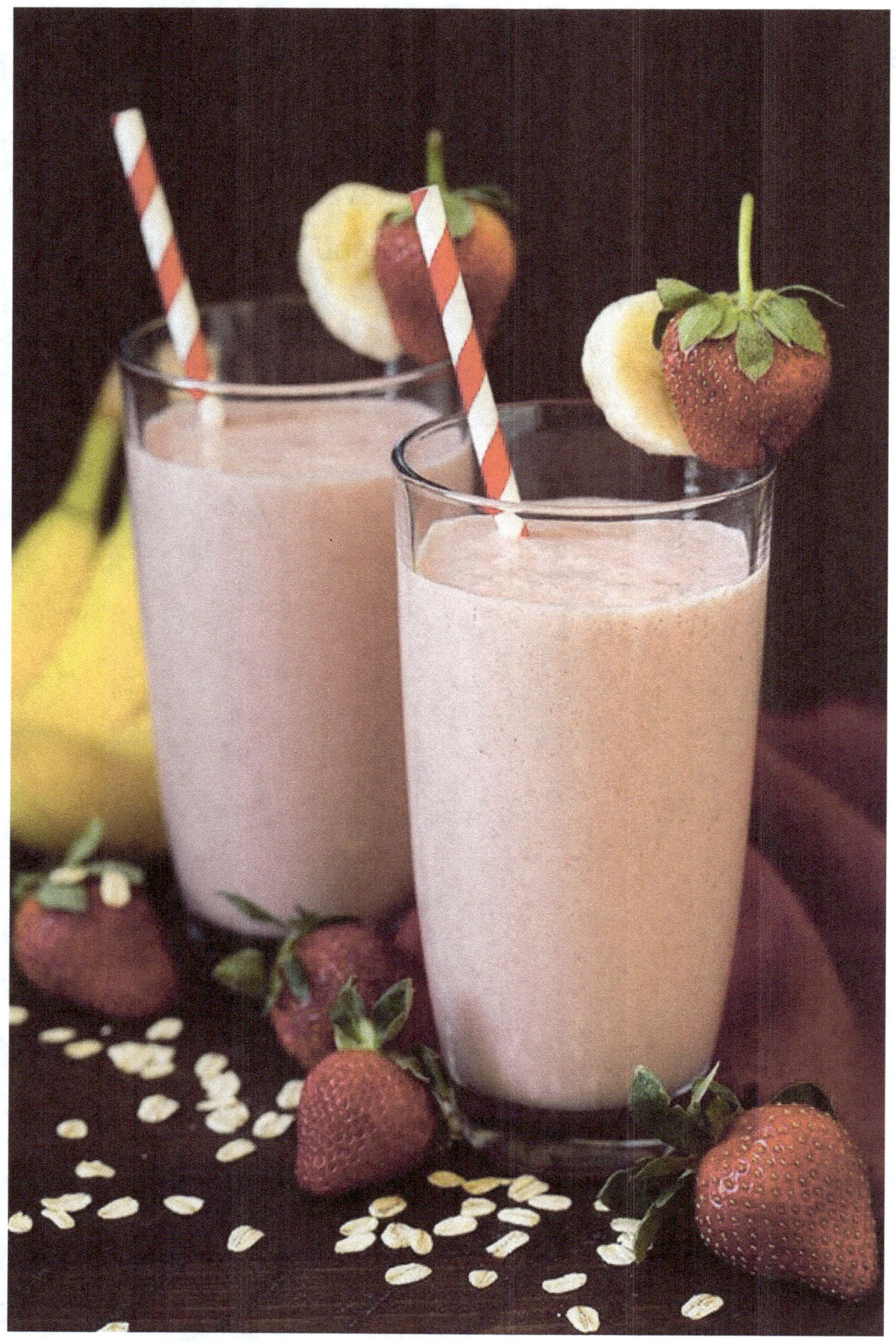

Preparation Time: 7 minutes

Servings: 2

Ingredients:

- 2 bananas
- 2 cups unsweetened coconut milk
- 2 cups plain Greek yogurt
- 1 cup frozen strawberries
- 2 teaspoons maple syrup

Preparation:

1. Add bananas, unsweetened coconut milk, strawberries, Greek yogurt, and maple syrup in a food processor.
2. Pulse to form a smooth mixture.
3. Take out and refrigerate.
4. Serve and enjoy!

Serving Suggestions: Top with banana slices before serving.

Variation Tip: You can also add strawberry syrup to enhance taste.

Nutritional Information per Serving:

Calories: 859| **Fat:** 60.6g| **Sat Fat:** 52.9g| **Carbohydrates:** 60.2g|

Fiber: 9.9g| **Sugar:** 37.9g| **Protein:** 29.8g

Johnny Rose Spinach Pear Smoothie

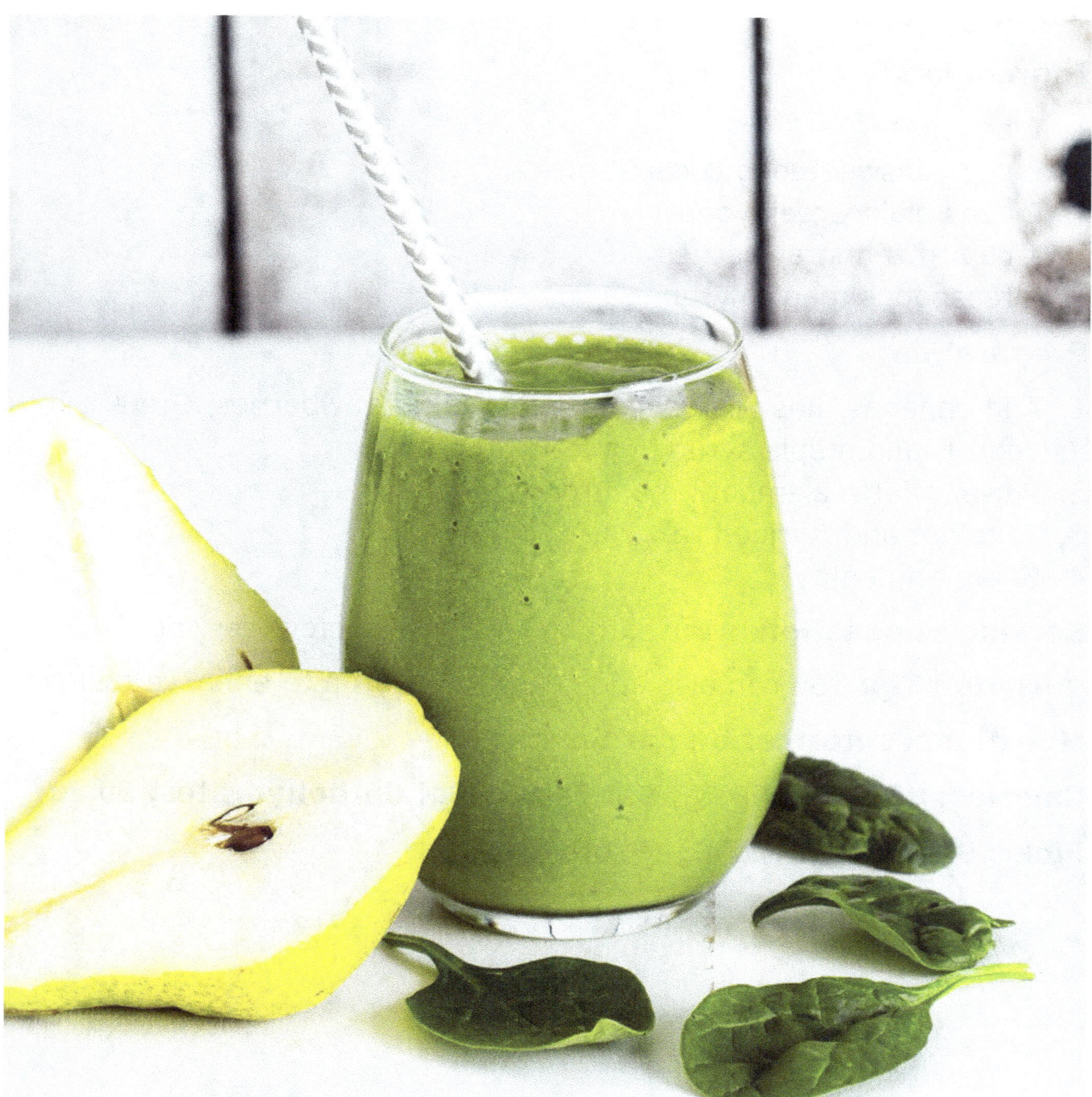

Preparation Time: 15 minutes
Servings: 4

Ingredients:

- 4 cups baby spinach

- 2 pears, cored and cut into chunks
- 3 cups unsweetened almond milk
- 1 cup boiling water
- 4 dates, pitted
- 2 bananas, cut into slices

Preparation:

1. Soak dates in a boiling water and set aside for about 10 minutes.
2. Add soaked dates along with soaking water in a high-speed blender.
3. Add in pears, baby spinach, almond milk, and bananas. Blend until a smooth mixture is formed.
4. Take out and refrigerate.
5. Serve and enjoy!

Serving Suggestions: Top with mint leaves before serving.

Variation Tip: You can also add maple syrup to enhance taste.

Nutritional Information per Serving:

Calories: 173| **Fat:** 3.1g| **Sat Fat:** 0.3g| **Carbohydrates:** 38.2g|

Fiber: 6.8g| **Sugar:** 22.8g| **Protein:** 2.8g

Moira Rose Kiwi Strawberry Smoothie

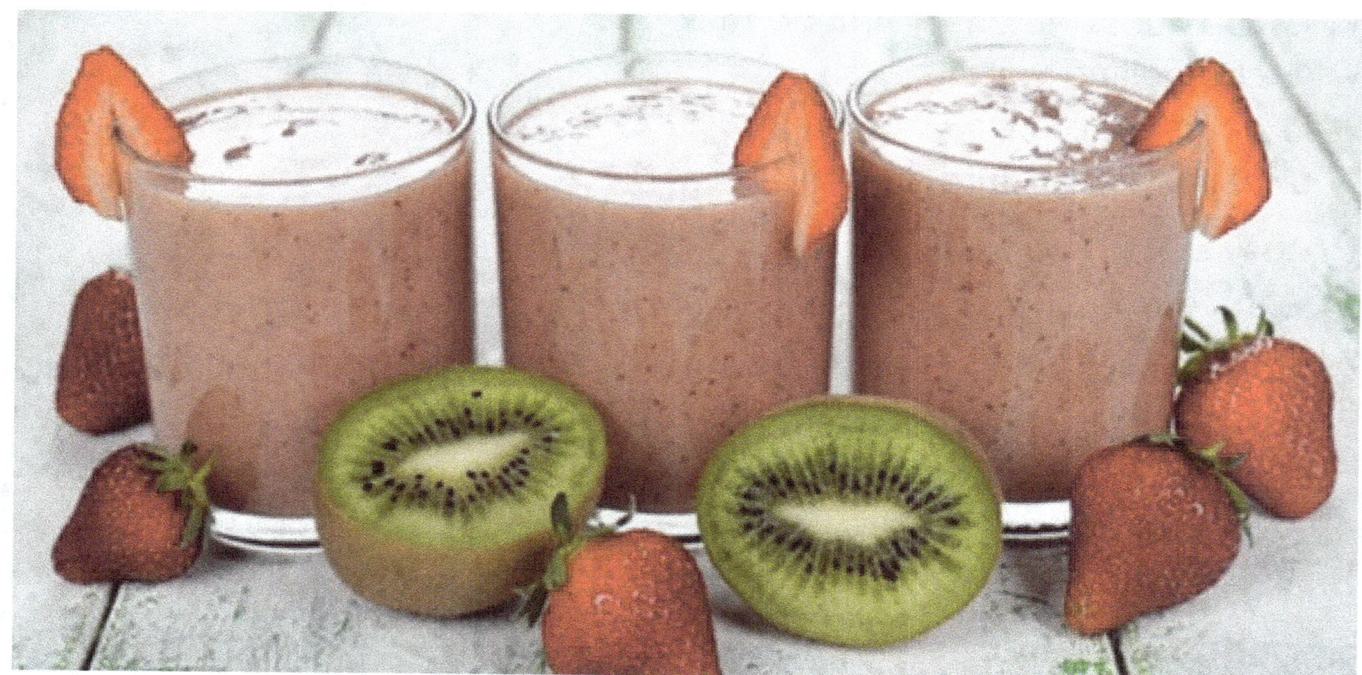

Preparation Time: 15 minutes

Servings: 4

Ingredients:

- 4 kiwis, peeled
- 1 cup unsweetened nut milk
- 2 cups frozen strawberries
- 2 cups fresh baby spinach

Preparation:

1. Add kiwi, nut milk, strawberries, and baby spinach in a food processor. Pulse until smooth.
2. Take out and top with strawberries and kiwi slices.
3. Serve and enjoy!

Serving Suggestions: Top with strawberry syrup and crushed ice before serving.

Variation Tip: You can add chia seeds to enhance taste.

Nutritional Information per Serving:

Calories: 122| **Fat:** 3g| **Sat Fat:** 1.3g| **Carbohydrates:** 23.9g|

Fiber: 4.4g| **Sugar:** 16.6g| **Protein:** 2.1g

David Rose Mango Chocolate Smoothie

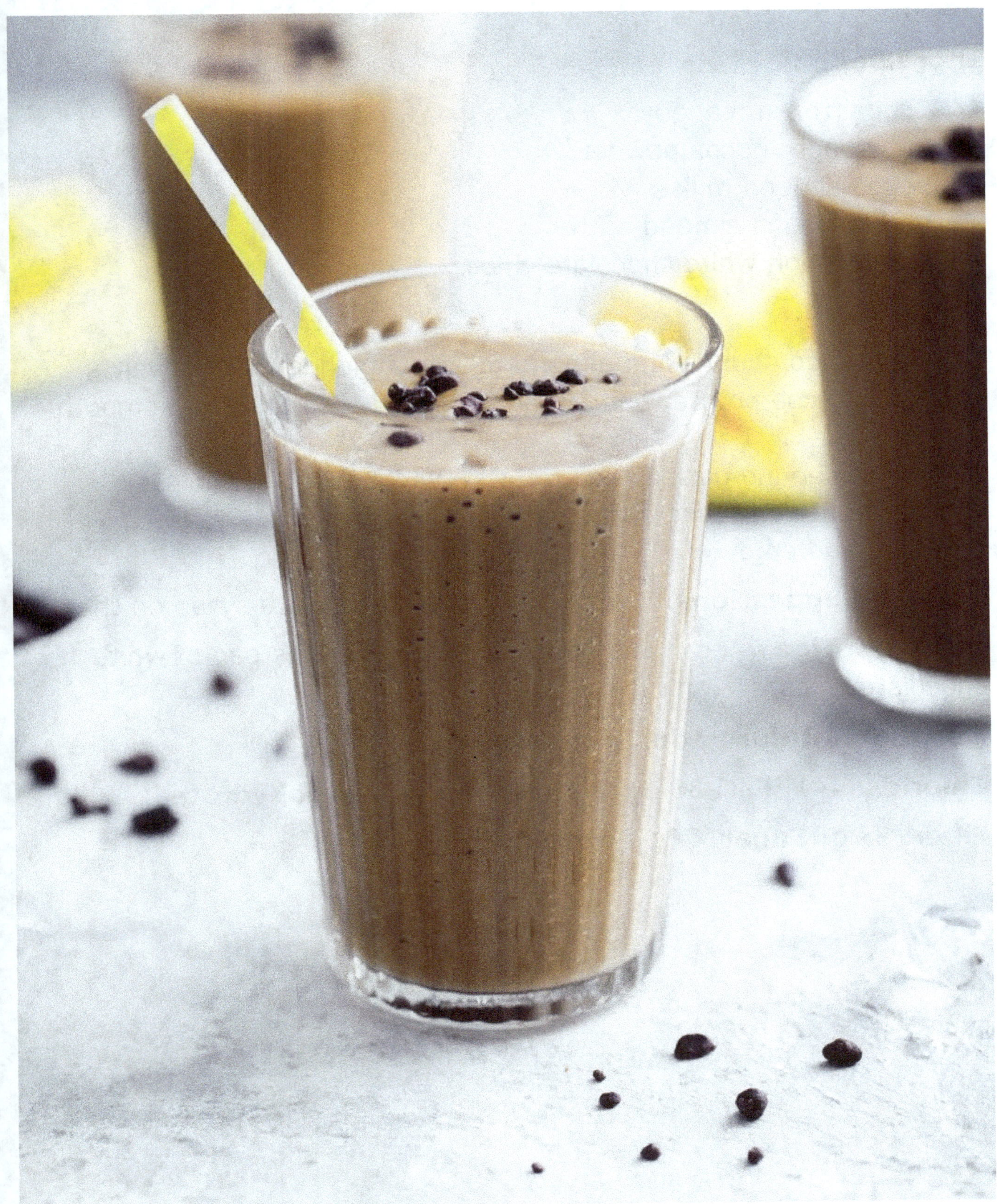

Preparation Time: 15 minutes
Servings: 4

Ingredients:

- 2 cups frozen mango
- 2 teaspoons cocoa powder
- 2 cups almond milk
- 2 tablespoons almond butter
- 1 tablespoon white chocolate chips

Preparation:

1. Add mango chunks and almond milk in a blender. Blend well.
2. Add in cocoa powder and almond butter. Blend to form a smooth mixture.
3. Pour in serving glasses and top with white chocolate chips.
4. Refrigerate and take out.
5. Serve and enjoy!

Serving Suggestions: You can serve with chocolate syrup on the top.

Variation Tip: You can use dark chocolate chips instead of white chocolate chips.

Nutritional Information per Serving:

Calories: 441| **Fat:** 36.6g| **Sat Fat:** 27.8g| **Carbohydrates:** 28.2g|
Fiber: 3.7g| **Sugar:** 20g| **Protein:** 6.8g

Shakes Recipes

Alexis Rose Strawberry Mango Milkshake

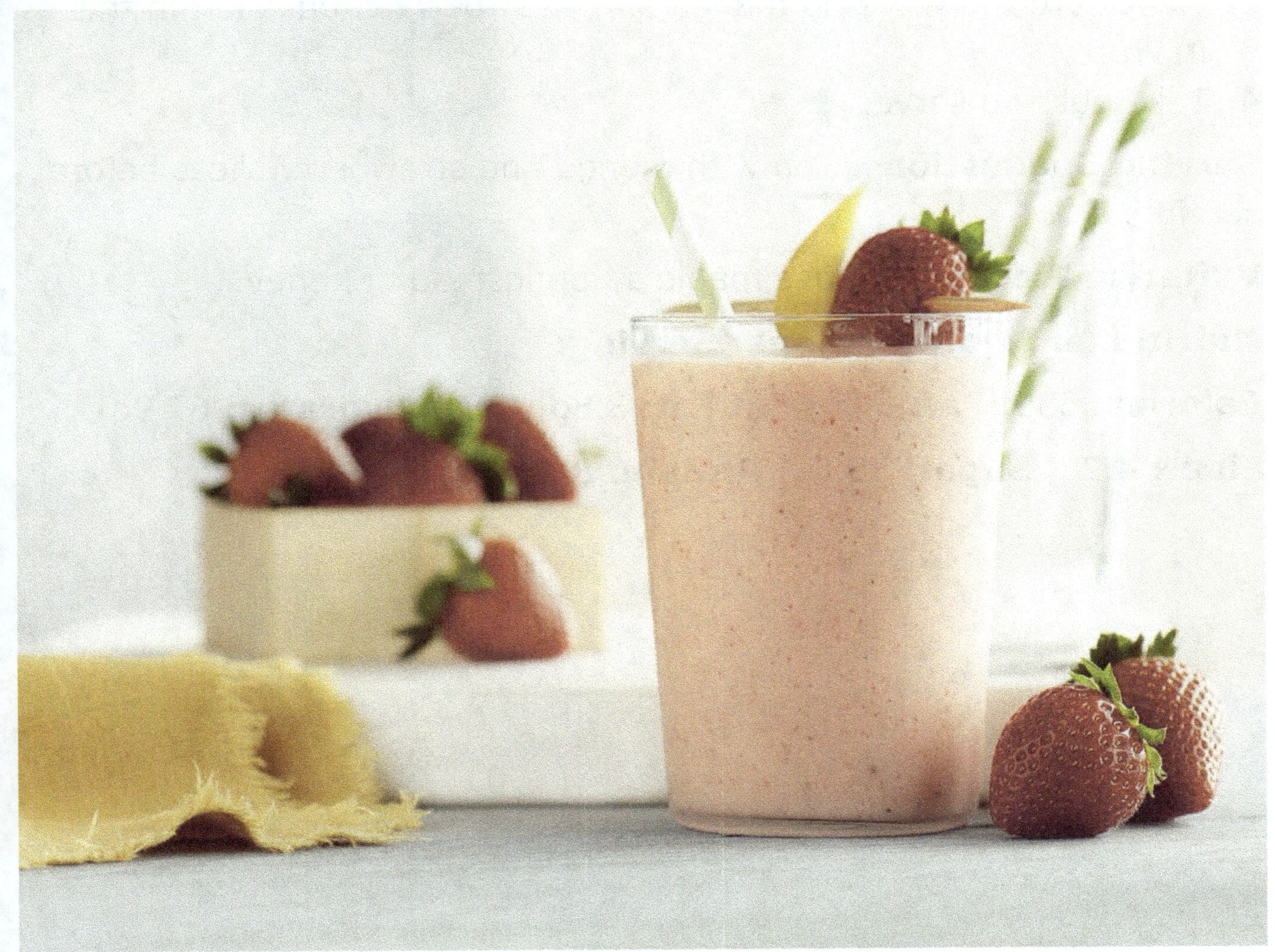

Preparation Time: 20 minutes
Servings: 4

Ingredients:

- 4 cups fresh strawberries
- 1 cup milk
- 2 cups chopped mangoes
- 3 cups vanilla frozen yogurt
- 3 tablespoons honey

Preparation:

1. Add milk and strawberries in a blender. Blend well.
2. Add in mangoes, frozen yogurt, and honey and blend properly.
3. Make sure there are no mango and strawberry chunks left in the mixture.
4. Take out and serve.

Serving Suggestions: Top with mango and strawberry slices before serving.

Variation Tip: You can use maple syrup instead of honey.

Nutritional Information per Serving:

Calories: 339| **Fat:** 6.5g| **Sat Fat:** 3.8g| **Carbohydrates:** 67.9g|

Fiber: 4.2g| **Sugar:** 53.5g| **Protein:** 8.2g

Jocelyn Schitt Chocolate Banana Milkshake

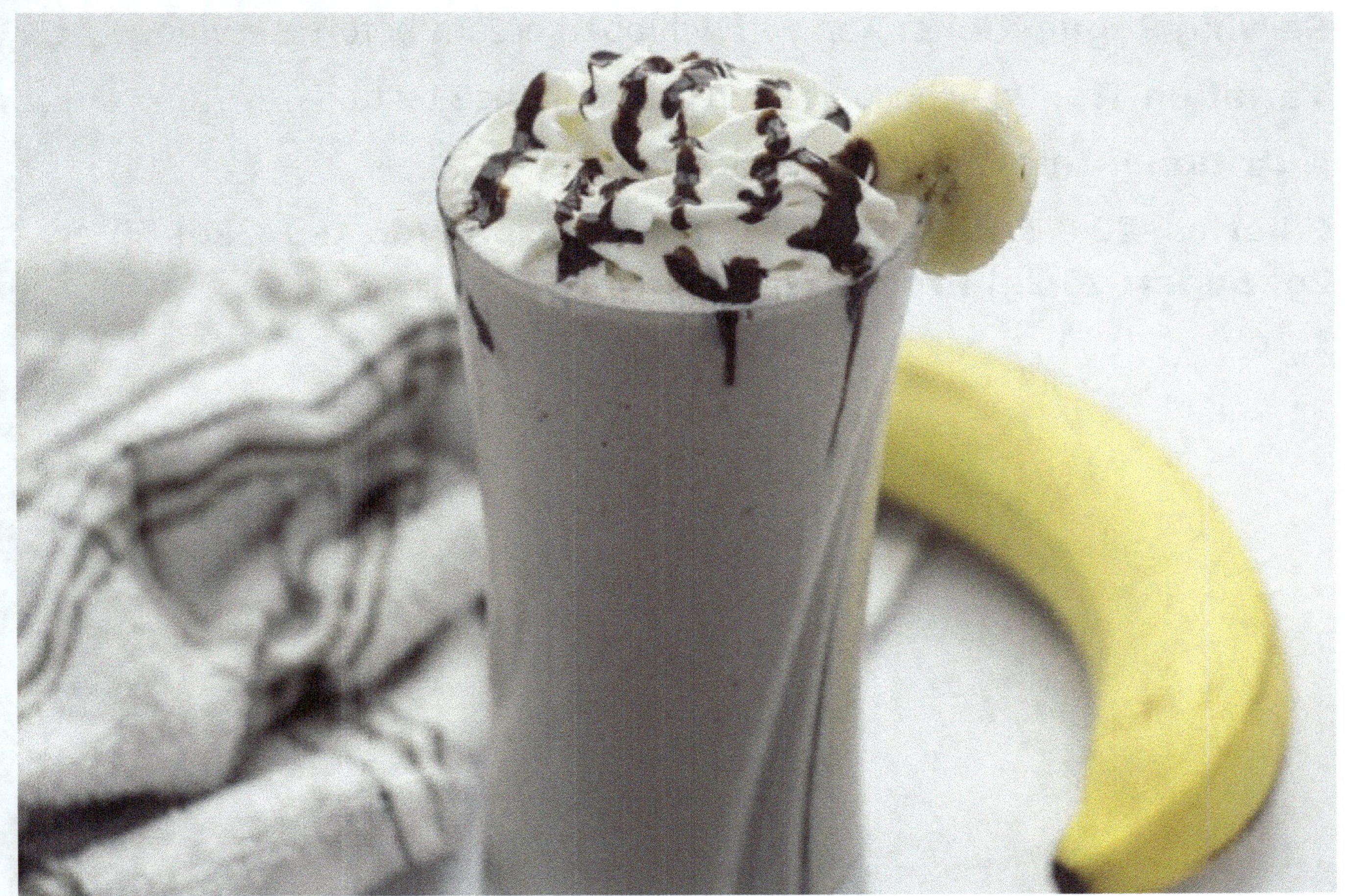

Preparation Time: 15 minutes
Servings: 4

Ingredients:

- 2 bananas
- 2 cups milk
- 1 cup powdered chocolate flavored malt drink mix
- 2 cups vanilla ice cream

Preparation:

1. Add bananas, milk, powdered chocolate, and vanilla in mixer.
2. Mix well until you are sure that there are no banana chunks left in the mixture.
3. Take out and top with chocolate chips.

4. Serve and enjoy!

Serving Suggestions: Top with whipped cream before serving.

Variation Tip: Use chocolate syrup to enhance taste.

Nutritional Information per Serving:

Calories: 204| **Fat:** 6.4g| **Sat Fat:** 4g| **Carbohydrates:** 32g| **Fiber:** 2g| **Sugar:** 23.2g| **Protein:** 6.1g

Mutt Schitt Avocado Milkshake

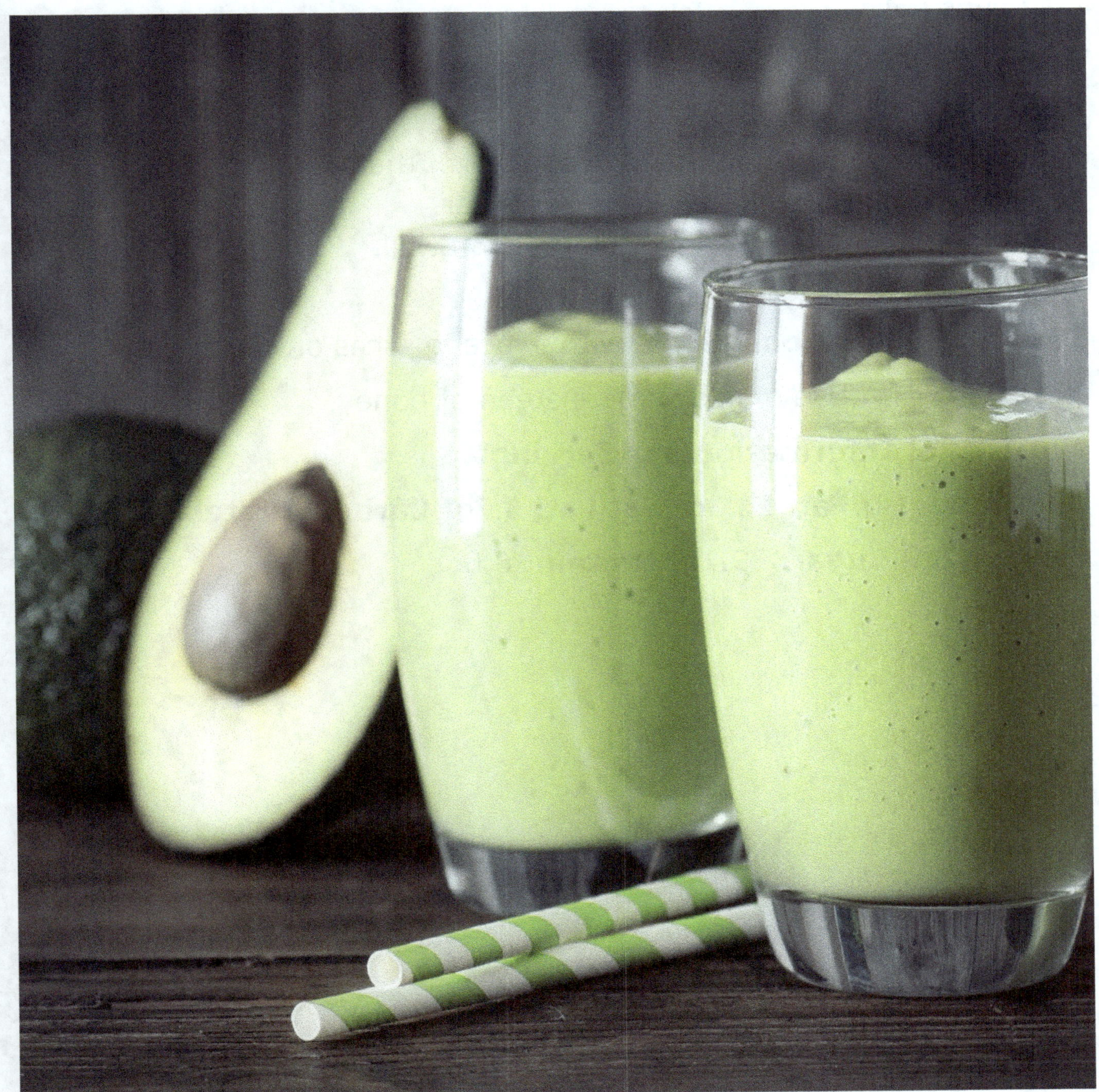

Preparation Time: 15 minutes
Servings: 4

Ingredients:

- 2 avocados

- 2 bananas
- 2 cups milk
- 6 tablespoons honey

Preparation:

1. Peel two avocados and take seeds out of them.
2. Slice them and add them in the blender.
3. Add in bananas, milk and honey. Blend well.
4. Take out and serve.

Serving Suggestions: Serve with avocado slices on the top.

Variation Tip: Use maple syrup instead of honey.

Nutritional Information per Serving:

Calories: 414| **Fat:** 22.3g| **Sat Fat:** 5.7g| **Carbohydrates:** 54.1g|

Fiber: 8.3g| **Sugar:** 39.1g| **Protein:** 6.6g

Stevie Budd Pineapple Coconut Milkshake

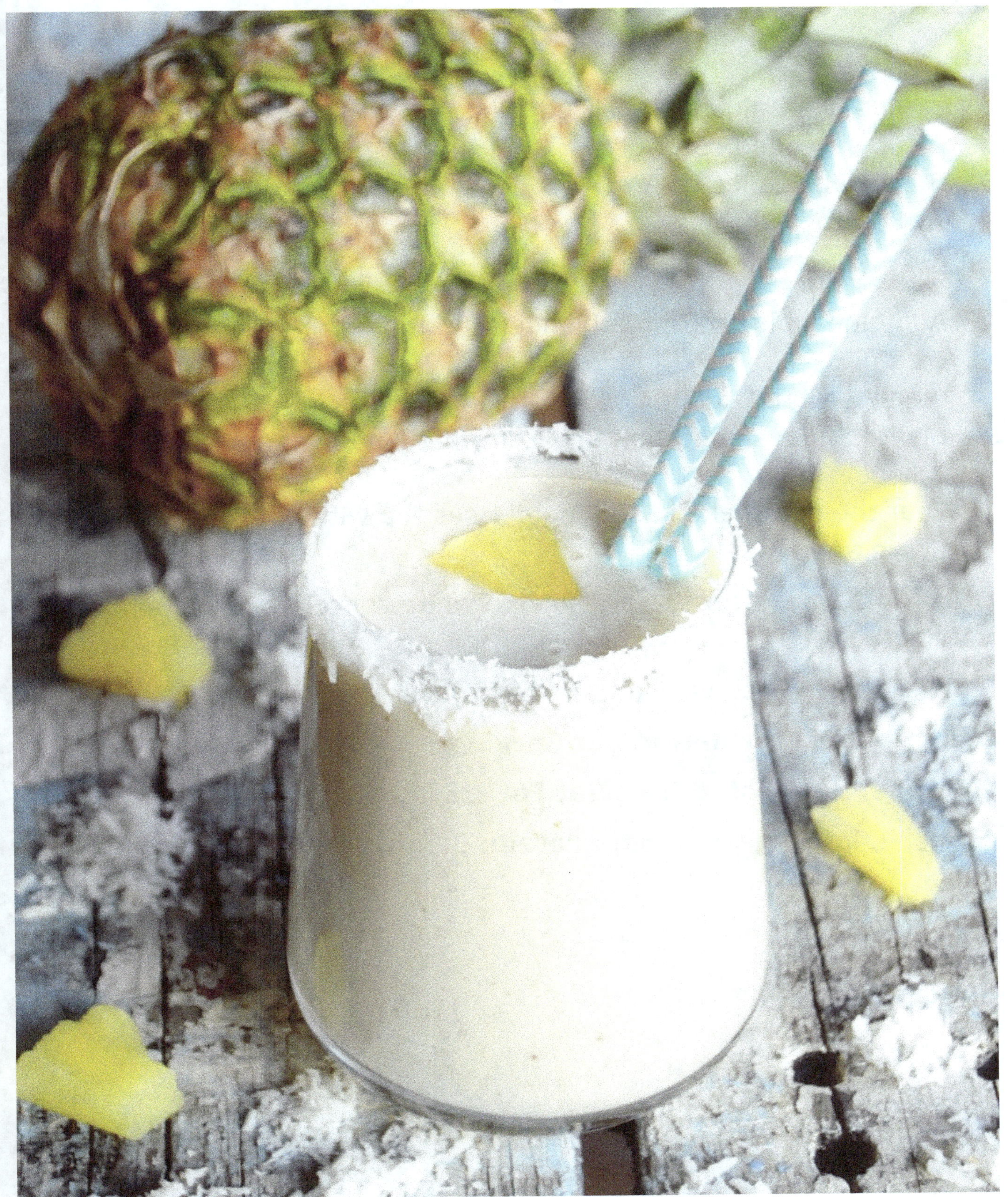

Preparation Time: 16 minutes
Servings: 6

Ingredients:

- 3 cups fresh pineapple, sliced
- 1 cup shredded coconut
- 3 cups vanilla ice cream
- 2 cups coconut milk

Preparation:

1. Add pineapple slices in a blender and top them with vanilla ice cream.
2. Blend well and add in coconut milk.
3. Blend until a smooth mixture is formed and mix in shredded coconut.
4. Pour the milkshake in serving glasses top with pineapple slices.
5. Serve and enjoy!

Serving Suggestions: Garnish with white chocolate chips before serving.

Variation Tip: Use vanilla essence for even better taste.

Nutritional Information per Serving:

Calories: 341| **Fat:** 27.1g| **Sat Fat:** 23.1g| **Carbohydrates:** 25.3g|
Fiber: 4.4g| **Sugar:** 18.6g| **Protein:** 3.9g

Roland Blueberry Milkshake

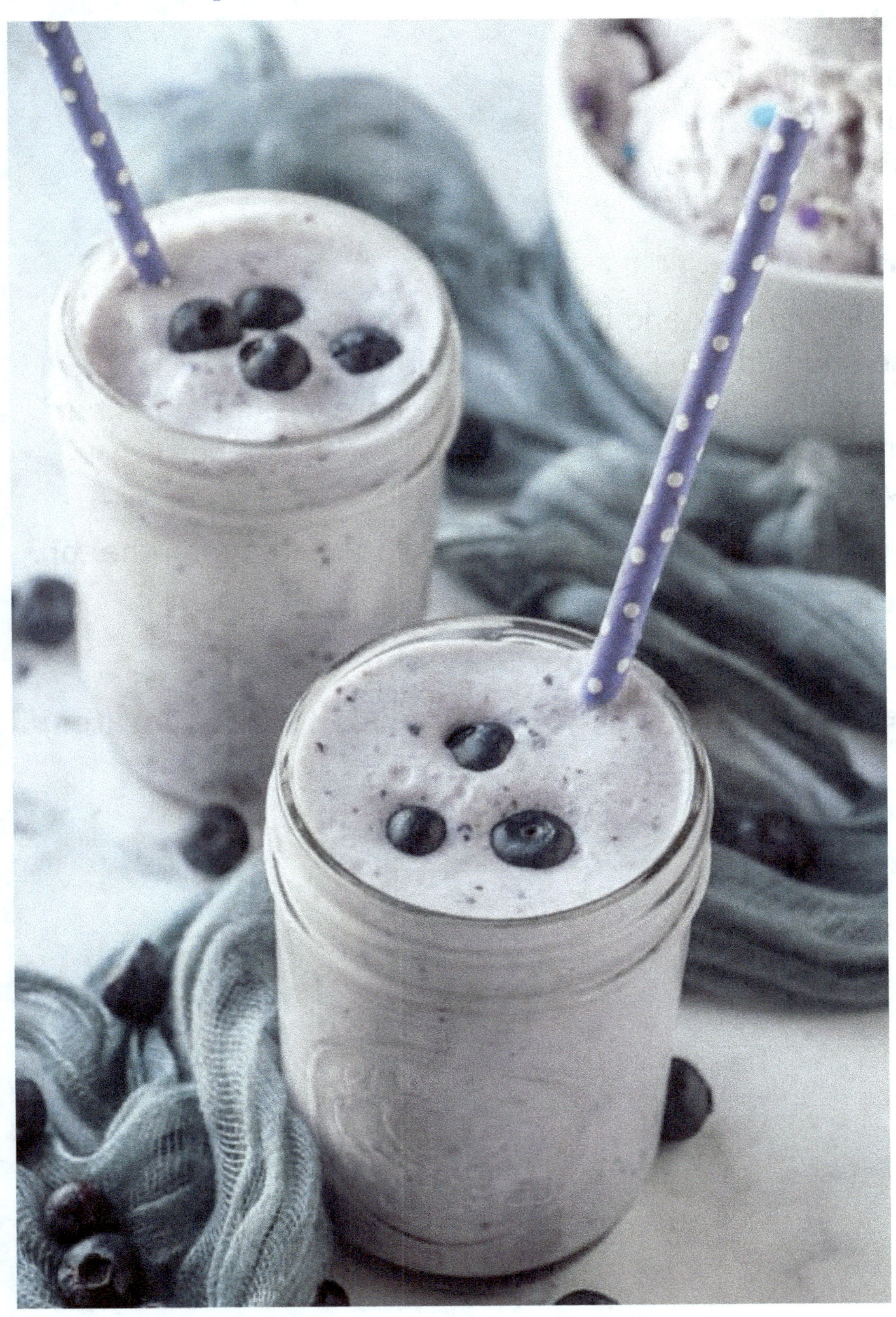

Preparation Time: 7 minutes
Servings: 2

Ingredients:

- 1 cup vanilla ice cream
- 1 cup blueberries
- 1 tablespoon honey
- 1 cup almond milk

Preparation:

1. Add almond milk and blueberries in a food processor.
2. Pulse and add vanilla ice cream and honey.
3. Pulse well until no blueberry chunks are left in the mixture.
4. Pour in serving glasses and top with fresh blueberries.
5. Serve and enjoy!

Serving Suggestions: Serve with whipped cream on the top.

Variation Tip: Add blueberry syrup to enhance taste.

Nutritional Information per Serving:

Calories: 418| **Fat:** 32.4g| **Sat Fat:** 27.6g| **Carbohydrates:** 33.8g|

Fiber: 4.7g| **Sugar:** 26.8g| **Protein:** 4.5g

Twyla Sands Pistachio Milkshake

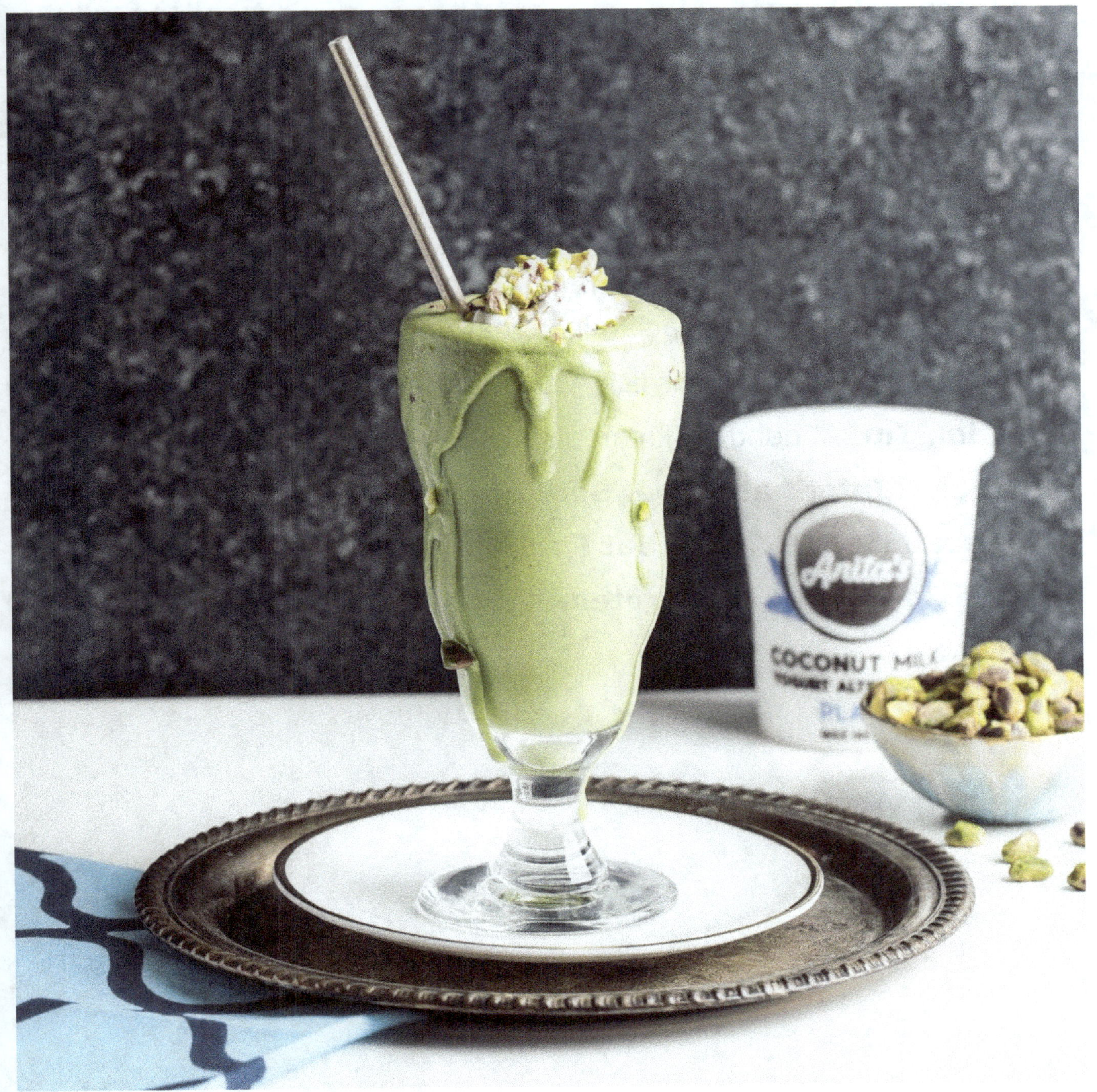

Preparation Time: 8 minutes
Servings: 2

Ingredients:

- 1 cup coconut milk

- 1 cup pistachio ice cream
- 2 teaspoons sugar
- ½ cup chopped pistachio
- ½ teaspoon cardamom powder

Preparation:

1. Add coconut milk, cardamom powder, chopped pistachio, sugar and ½ cup pistachio ice cream in a food processor.
2. Blend well and take out in serving glasses.
3. Top with remaining pistachio ice cream and serve.

Serving Suggestions: Garnish with chopped pistachio before serving.

Variation Tip: Almond milk can also be used.

Nutritional Information per Serving:

Calories: 663| **Fat:** 55.7g| **Sat Fat:** 37.1g| **Carbohydrates:** 37g|

Fiber: 5.3g| **Sugar:** 28g| **Protein:** 10.8g

Robert Currie Mint Chocolate Milkshake

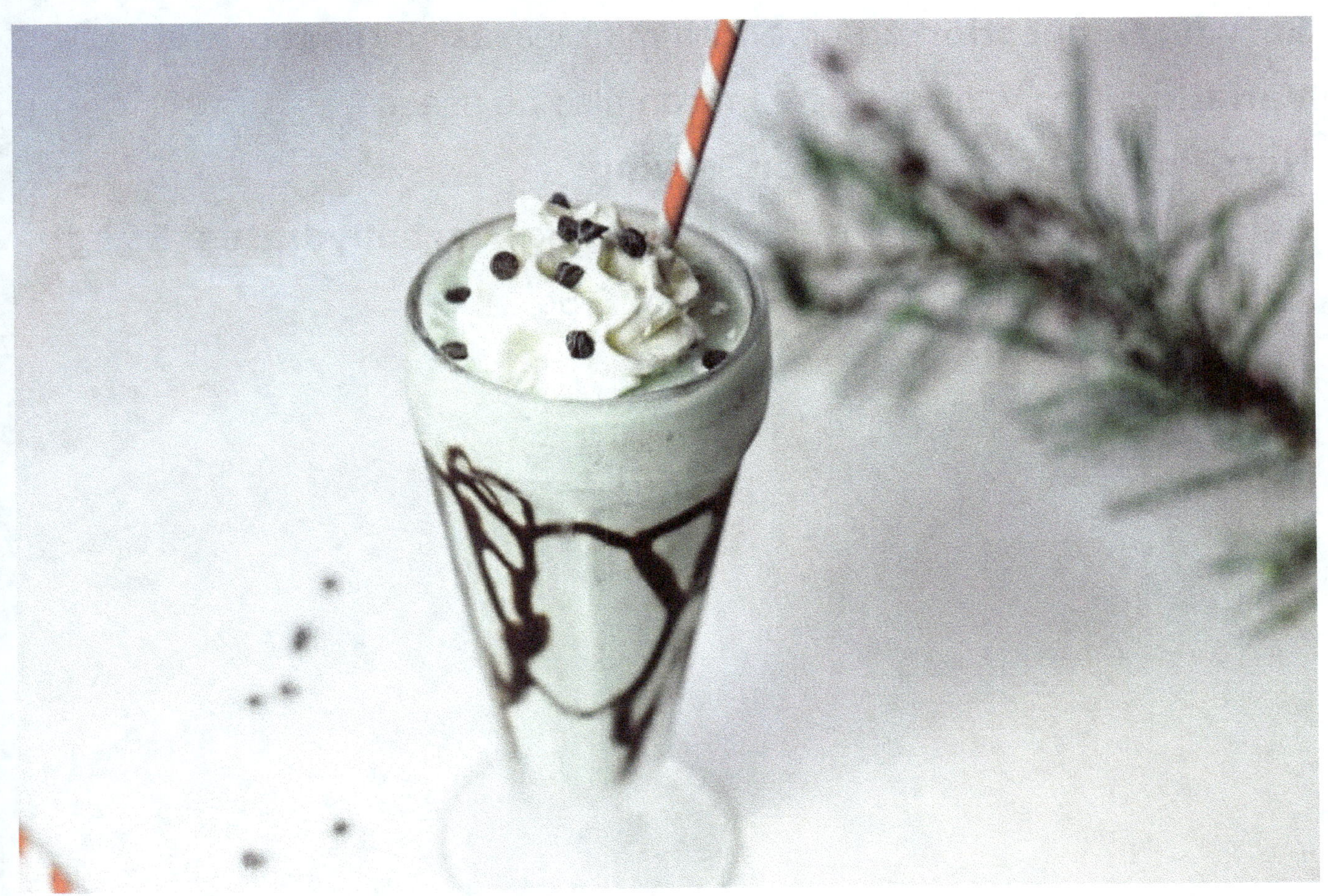

Preparation Time: 12 minutes
Servings: 3

Ingredients:

- 1 cup coconut milk
- ½ cup chocolate syrup
- 1 cup mint ice cream
- 3 drops peppermint extract
- 3 teaspoons chocolate chips

Preparation:

1. Add coconut milk, chocolate syrup and peppermint extract in a blender. Blend well.
2. Take out and add in mint ice cream.

3. Top with chocolate chips and serve.

Serving Suggestions: Serve with mint leaves on the top.

Variation Tip: Vanilla ice cream can also be used.

Nutritional Information per Serving:

Calories: 489| **Fat:** 28.7g| **Sat Fat:** 22.6g| **Carbohydrates:** 55.1g|

Fiber: 3.2g| **Sugar:** 44.6g| **Protein:** 6.5g

Veronica Lee Marshmallow Milkshake

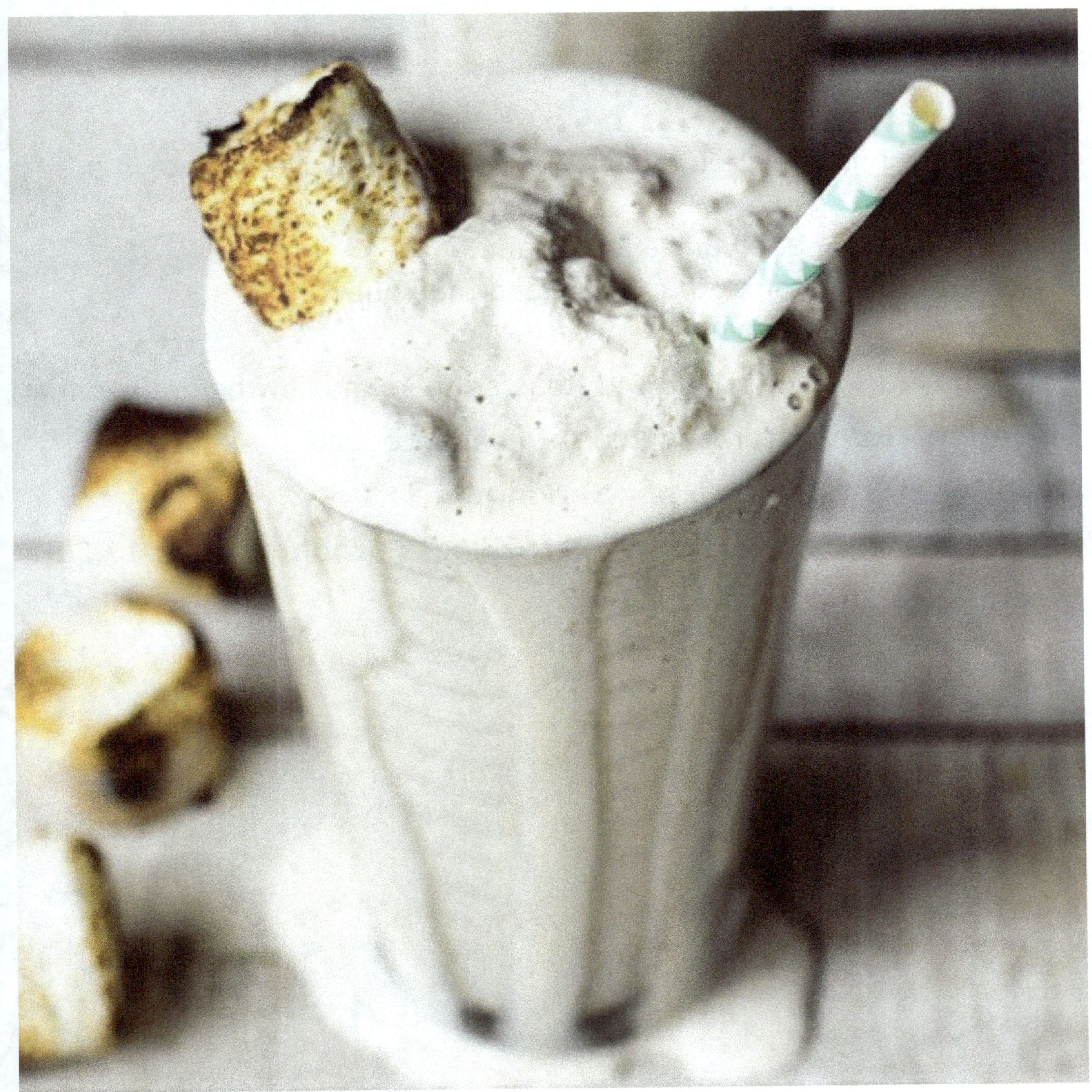

Preparation Time: 15 minutes
Servings: 8

Ingredients:

- 2 cups marshmallow crème

- 4 cups vanilla ice cream
- 4 cups coconut milk
- 2 teaspoons vanilla extract

Preparation:

1. Add marshmallow crème, coconut milk, and vanilla extract in a blender.
2. Blend well and add vanilla ice cream.
3. Blend to form a smooth mixture and take out.
4. Refrigerate and serve.

Serving Suggestions: Top with toasted marshmallow before serving.

Variation Tip: You can add honey to enhance taste.

Nutritional Information per Serving:

Calories: 358| **Fat:** 32.1g| **Sat Fat:** 27.6g| **Carbohydrates:** 17.5g| **Fiber:** 2.9g| **Sugar:** 13.4g| **Protein:** 3.9g

Juice Recipes

Theodore Mullens Mango Pineapple Juice

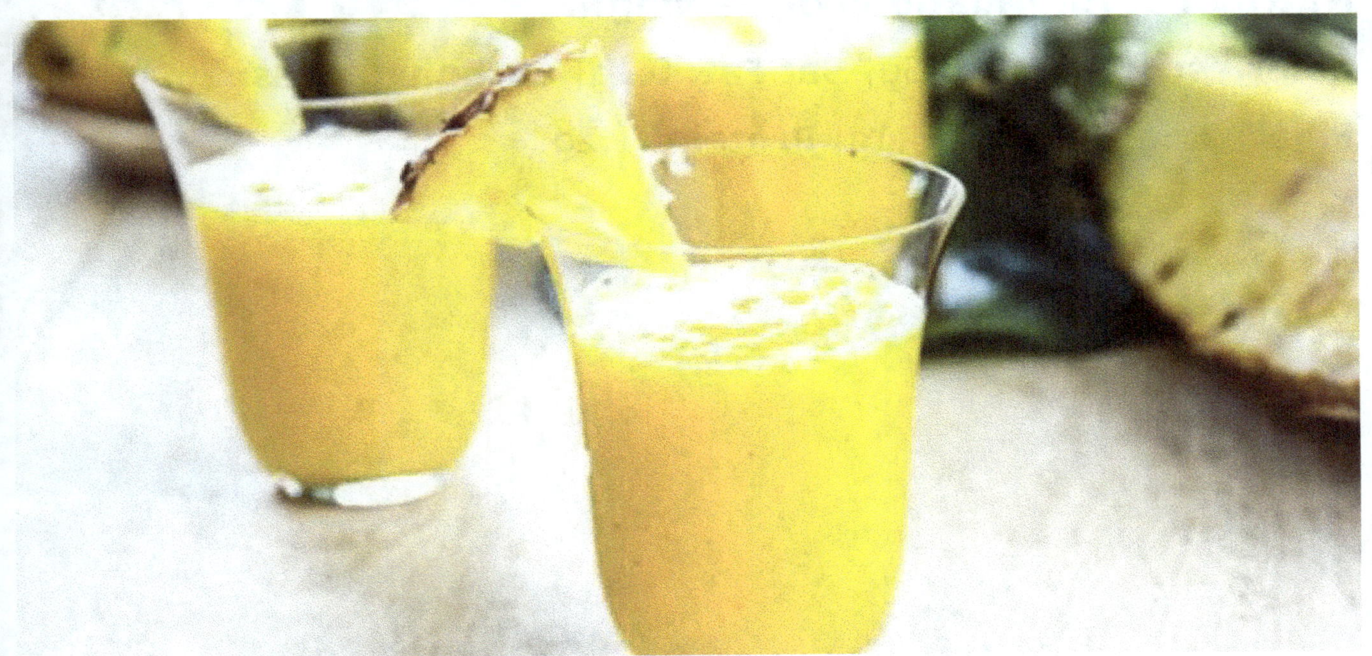

Preparation Time: 12 minutes
Servings: 6

Ingredients:

- 4 cups chopped mangoes
- 2 cups chopped pineapple
- 4 cups water
- 1 teaspoon lemon juice
- 4 teaspoons sugar

Preparation:

1. Add mango chunks, pineapple chunks, and water in a high-speed blender. Blend well.
2. Add in sugar and lemon juice. Blend until no chunk is left in the juice.
3. Add in more water if required and take out the juice.
4. Serve and enjoy!

Serving Suggestions: Serve with chilled mango and pineapple slices.

Variation Tip: Use honey instead of sugar.

Nutritional Information per Serving:

Calories: 104| **Fat:** 0.5g| **Sat Fat:** 0.1g| **Carbohydrates:** 26.4g|

Fiber: 2.5g| **Sugar:** 23.1g| **Protein:** 1.2g

Patrick Brewer Cucumber Apple Kiwi Juice

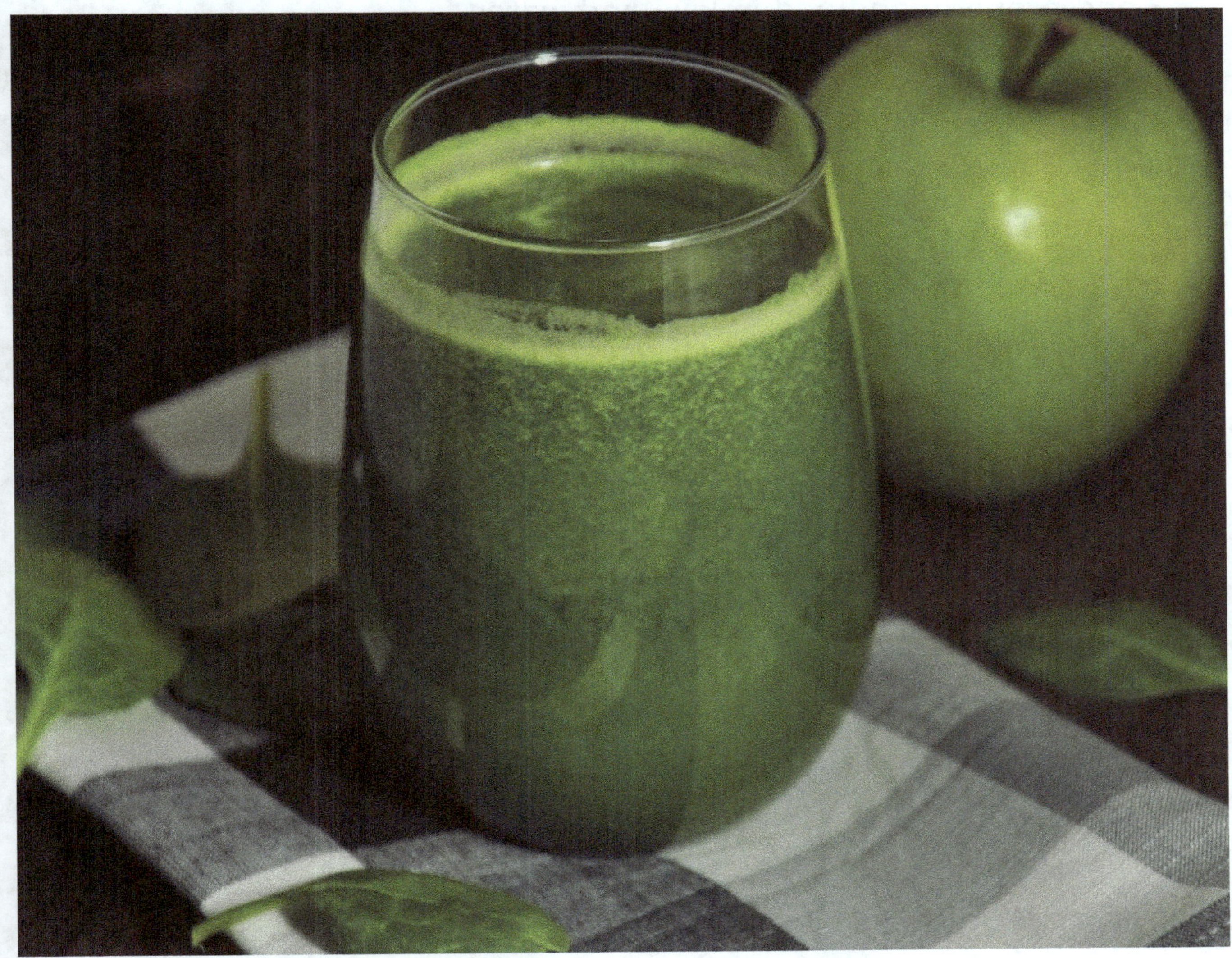

Preparation Time: 10 minutes
Servings: 6

Ingredients:

- 4 cucumbers, sliced
- 4 green apples, sliced
- 6 kiwis, peeled and sliced
- 3 cups water
- 4 teaspoons sugar

Preparation:

1. Add apples, cucumbers, and sugar in a high-speed blender.
2. Blend properly and add in kiwi and water.
3. Blend and add in more water if required.
4. Pour out the juice and serve.

Serving Suggestions: Serve with mint leaves and ice.

Variation Tip: Add a pinch of black pepper to enhance taste.

Nutritional Information per Serving:

Calories: 164| **Fat:** 0.9g| **Sat Fat:** 0.1g| **Carbohydrates:** 41.6g|

Fiber: 6.9g| **Sugar:** 28.3g| **Protein:** 2.6g

Johnny Rose Carrot Orange Juice

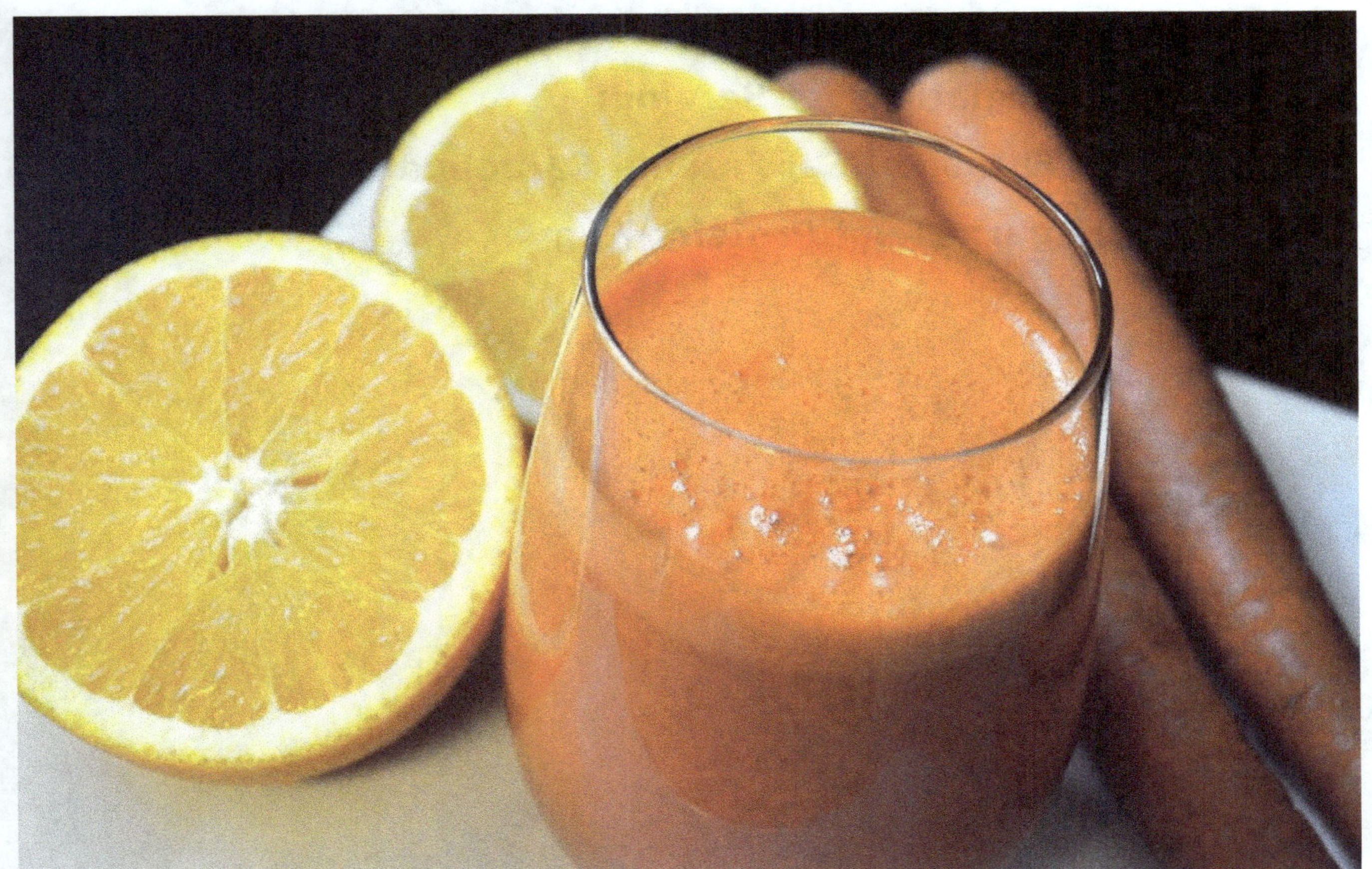

Preparation Time: 10 minutes
Servings: 5

Ingredients:

- 7 cups chopped carrots
- 4 oranges
- 2 cups water
- ½ teaspoon black pepper

Preparation:

1. Peel four oranges and take out its pulp.
2. Meanwhile, add carrots and water in a blender and blend well.
3. Combine orange pulp and carrot juice.
4. Add in black pepper and mix well.
5. Serve and enjoy!

Serving Suggestions: Serve with chopped mint leaves on the top.

Variation Tip: You can also use white pepper.

Nutritional Information per Serving:

Calories: 133| **Fat:** 0.2g| **Sat Fat:** 0g| **Carbohydrates:** 32.6g|

Fiber: 7.4g| **Sugar:** 21.3g| **Protein:** 2.7g

Moira Rose Watermelon Juice

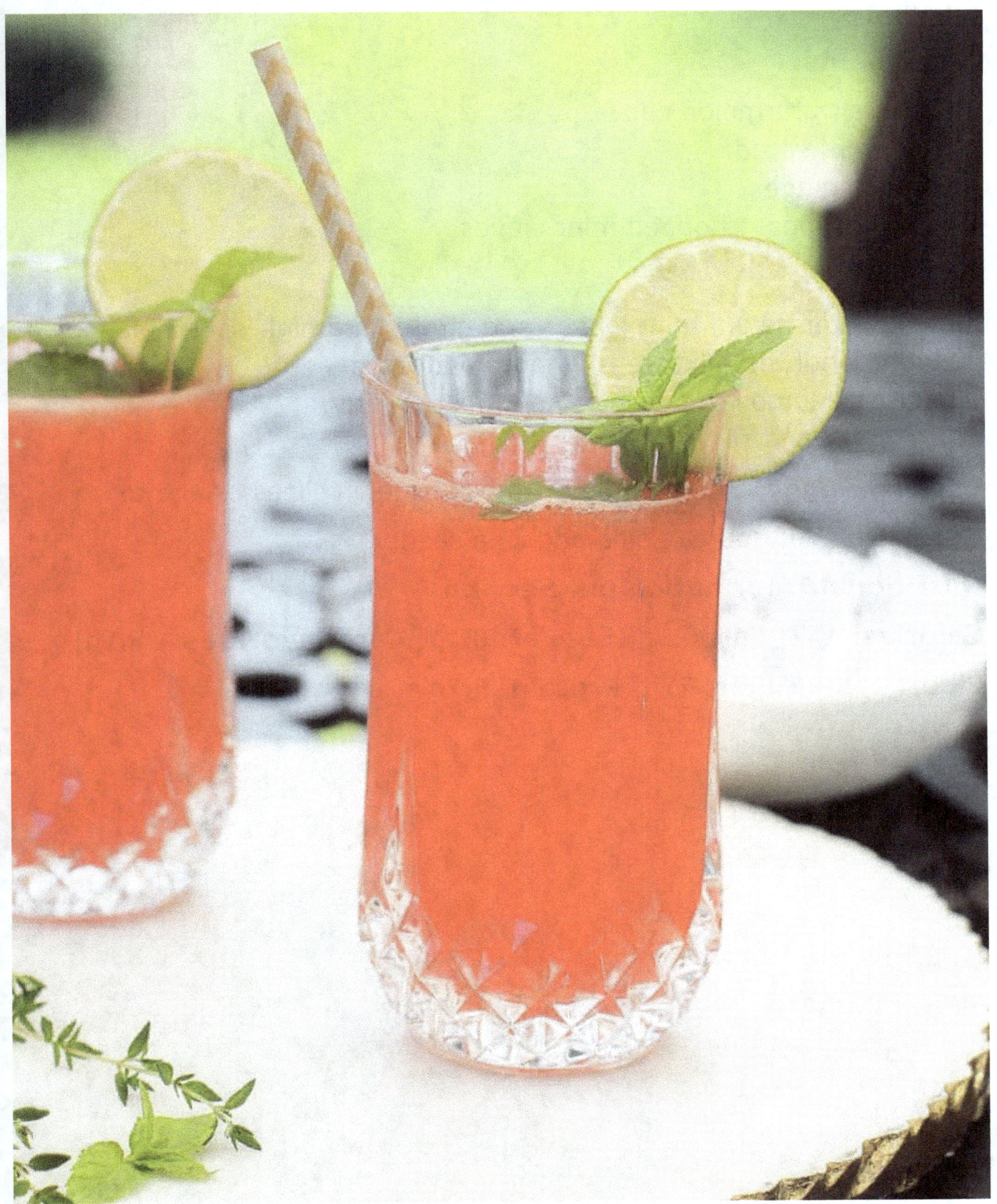

Preparation Time: 5 minutes
Servings: 1

Ingredients:

- 3 cups watermelon cubes
- 1 lemon, sliced
- ½ inch ginger
- 2 tablespoons chopped mint leaves

Preparation:

1. Add watermelon, mint leaves and ginger in a high-speed blender.
2. Blend until the mixture is smooth and frothy.
3. Squeeze lemon in the juice and mix properly.
4. Take out and serve.

Serving Suggestions: Serve with watermelon slices on the top.

Variation Tip: You can also add chia seeds.

Nutritional Information per Serving:

Calories: 152| **Fat:** 0.9g| **Sat Fat:** 0.1g| **Carbohydrates:** 38.5g|

Fiber: 4.2g| **Sugar:** 27g| **Protein:** 3.7g

David Rose Sugarcane Juice

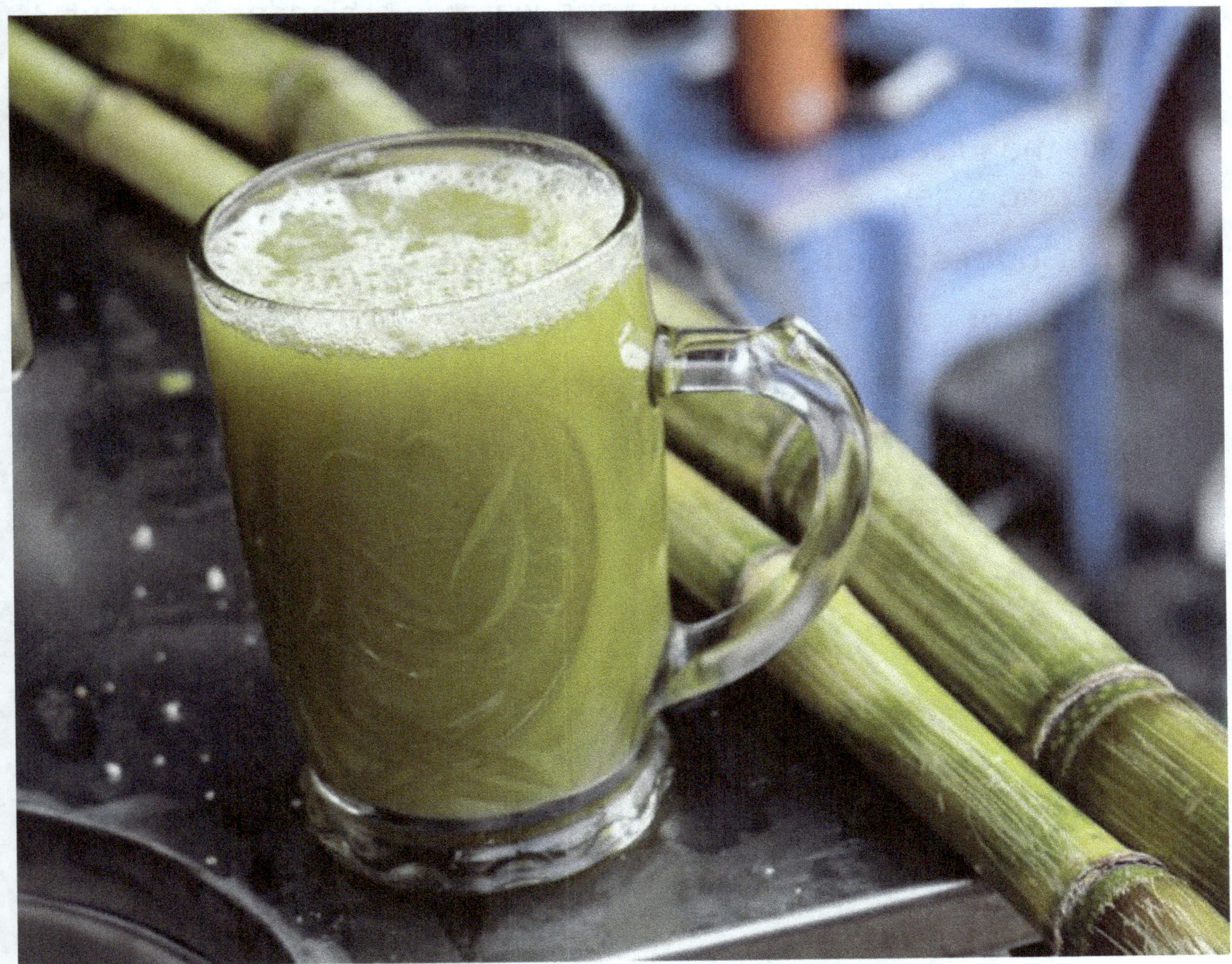

Preparation Time: 10 minutes
Cooking Time: 3 minutes
Servings: 4

Ingredients:

- 2 sugarcane sticks
- ½ cup water
- 1 inch ginger
- 1 lemon

Preparation:

1. Peel the thick skin of sugarcane and cut it into small pieces.
2. Meanwhile, blend ginger, lemon and water in a blender for about 3 minutes.
3. Add in sugar cane pieces and blend well.
4. Strain the juice and pour it in serving glasses.
5. Serve and enjoy!

Serving Suggestions: Serve with mint leaves on the top.

Variation Tip: You can omit lemon if you want.

Nutritional Information per Serving:

Calories: 106| **Fat:** 0.1g| **Sat Fat:** 0g| **Carbohydrates:** 27.7g|

Fiber: 0.5g| **Sugar:** 20.4g| **Protein:** 0.2g

Alexis Rose Mint Juice

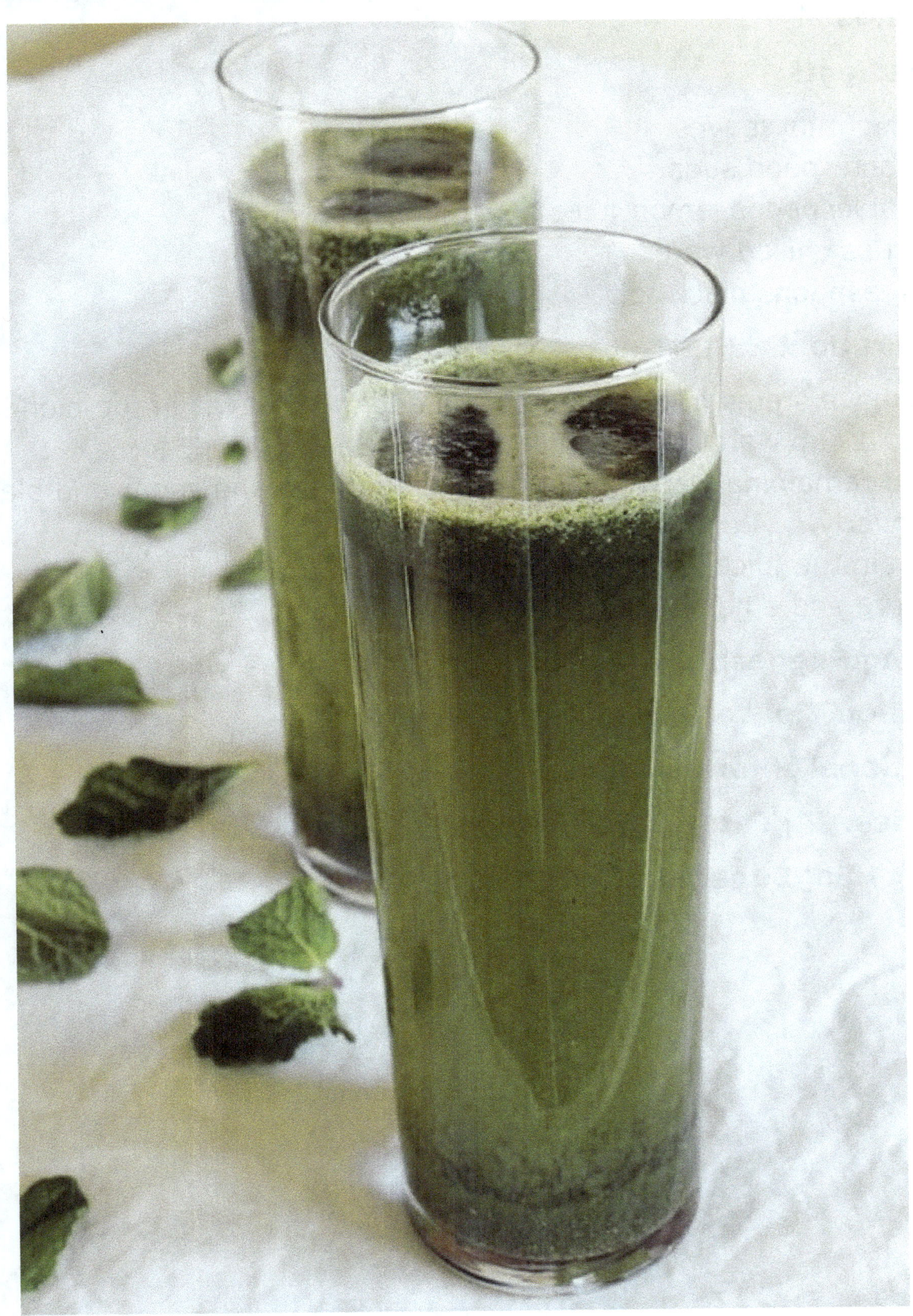

Preparation Time: 15 minutes
Servings: 4

Ingredients:

- 1 cup mint leaves
- 1 tablespoon sugar
- 3 tablespoons lemon juice
- 5 cups chilled water
- 2 teaspoons black salt

Preparation:

1. Remove stems of mint leaves and add mint leaves in the blender.
2. Add 1 cup water and blend until a puree is formed.
3. Add remaining water, black salt, lemon juice and sugar and blend properly.
4. Strain the juice and top with mint leaves.
5. Serve and enjoy!

Serving Suggestions: Add crushed ice before serving.

Variation Tip: You can replace sugar with honey.

Nutritional Information per Serving:

Calories: 24| **Fat:** 0.3g| **Sat Fat:** 0.1g| **Carbohydrates:** 5.2g|

Fiber: 1.6g| **Sugar:** 3.2g| **Protein:** 0.8g

Jocelyn Schitt Coconut Juice

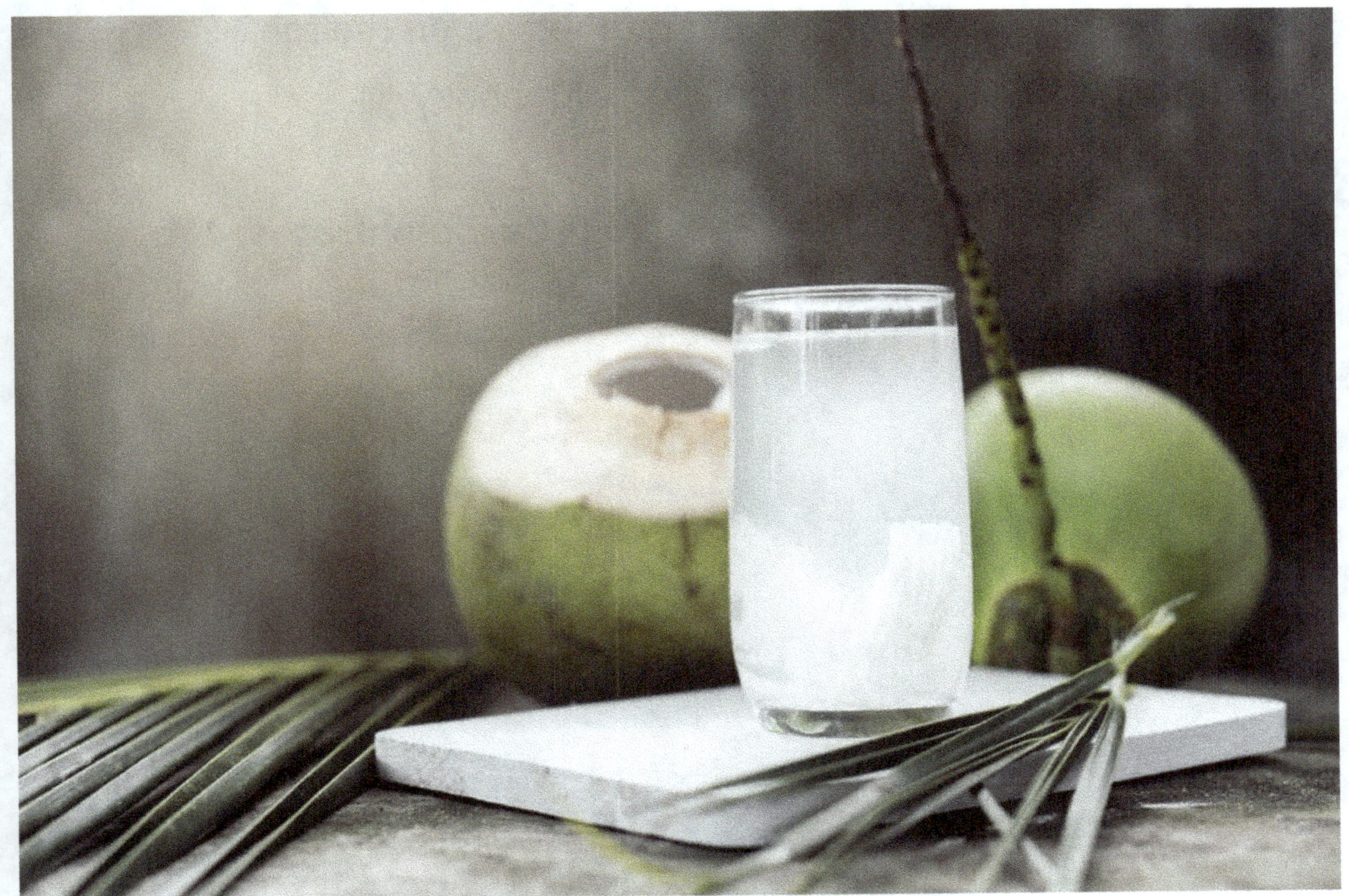

Preparation Time: 6 minutes
Servings: 2

Ingredients:

- 2 cups coconut water
- 2 teaspoons sugar
- ½ cup tender coconut
- ½ cup shredded coconut

Preparation:

1. Add coconut water, sugar, shredded coconut and tender coconut in a blender.
2. Blend properly until coconut is fully blended with the coconut water.
3. Pour coconut juice in serving glasses and put them in refrigerator.

4. Take out and serve.

Serving Suggestions: Serve with crushed ice on the top.

Variation Tip: Sugar can be replaced with honey.

Nutritional Information per Serving:

Calories: 137| **Fat:** 7.2g| **Sat Fat:** 6.3g| **Carbohydrates:** 17g|

Fiber: 5.5g| **Sugar:** 11.5g| **Protein:** 2.8g

Mutt Schitt Cherry Juice

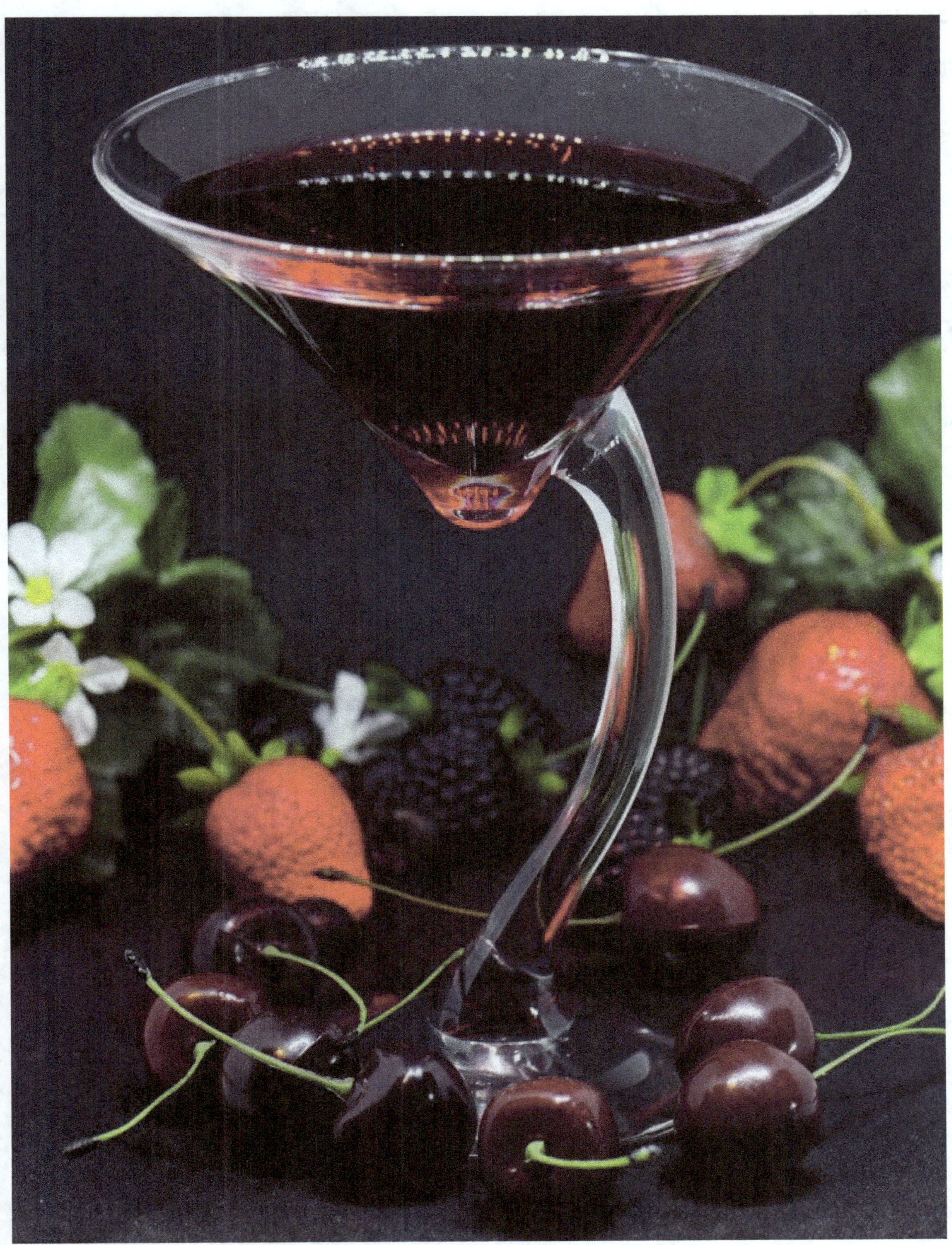

Preparation Time: 15 minutes
Servings: 4

Ingredients:

- 1½ cups cherries
- 1½ plums
- 1 cup diced watermelon
- 1 cup water
- ½ teaspoon black salt

Preparation:

1. Remove cherry seeds and boil cherries and plums for 2 minutes.
2. Immediately add them in cold water for few minutes and remove their skin.
3. Add cherries, plums, watermelon, water and black salt in a food processor.
4. Pulse well and take out.
5. Top with crushed ice and serve.

Serving Suggestions: Top with cherry before serving.

Variation Tip: Use black pepper for an even better taste.

Nutritional Information per Serving:

Calories: 170| **Fat:** 0.4g| **Sat Fat:** 0g| **Carbohydrates:** 42.3g|

Fiber: 2g| **Sugar:** 12g| **Protein:** 1.3g

Tea Recipes

Stevie Budd Black Tea

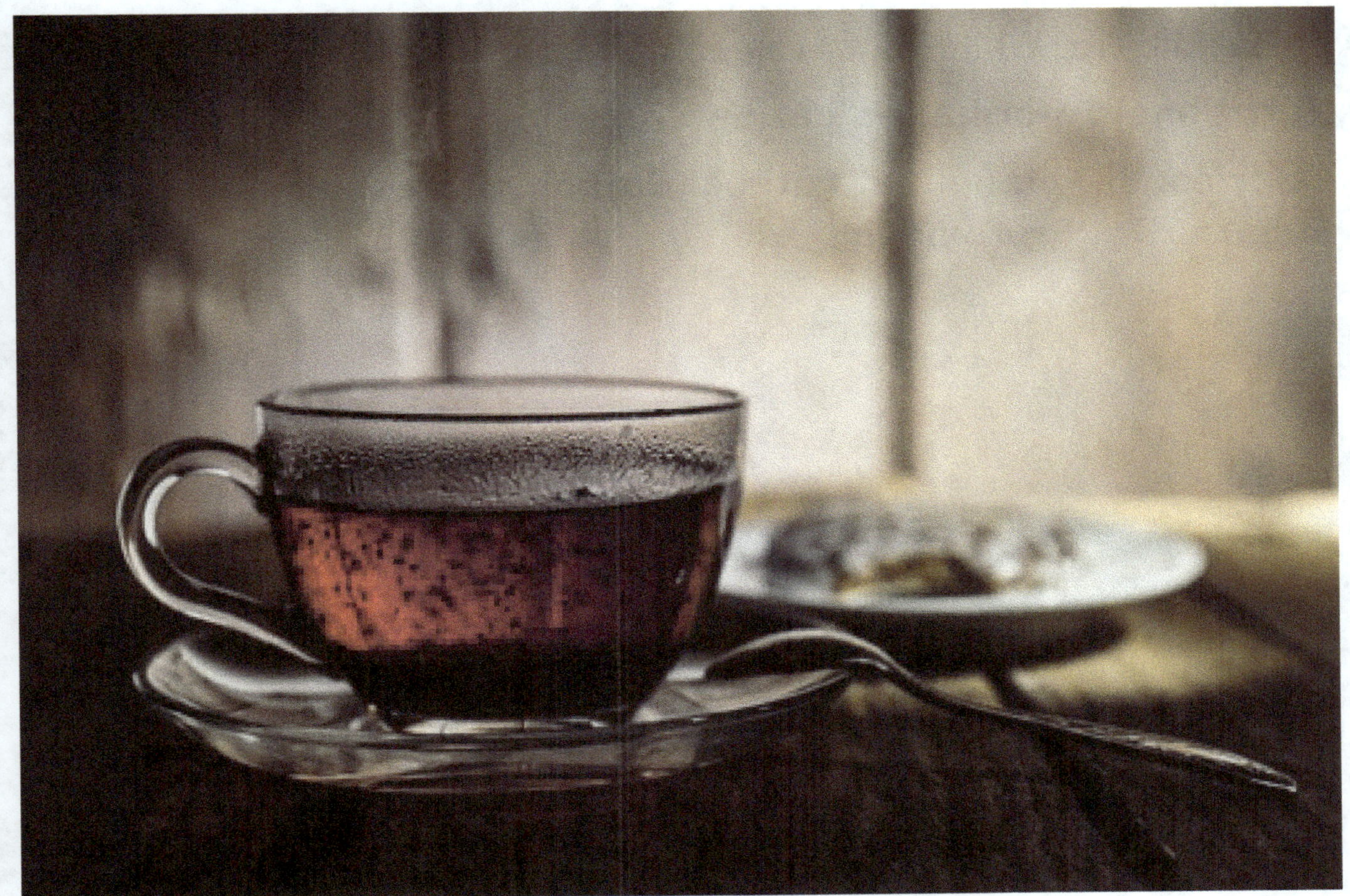

Preparation Time: 6 minutes
Cooking Time: 5 minutes
Servings: 4

Ingredients:

- 2 teaspoons tea
- 4 cups water
- Brown sugar, to taste

Preparation:

1. Add tea and water in a pan and boil it.
2. Cover the lid and cook for about 5 minutes.

3. Take out and add in brown sugar.
4. Serve and enjoy!

Serving Suggestions: Serve with some snacks.

Variation Tip: White sugar can also be used.

Nutritional Information per Serving:

Calories: 3| **Fat:** 0g| **Sat Fat:** 0g| **Carbohydrates:** 0.8g| **Fiber:** 0g| **Sugar:** 0.7g| **Protein:** 0g

Roland Schitt Ginger Lemon Black Tea

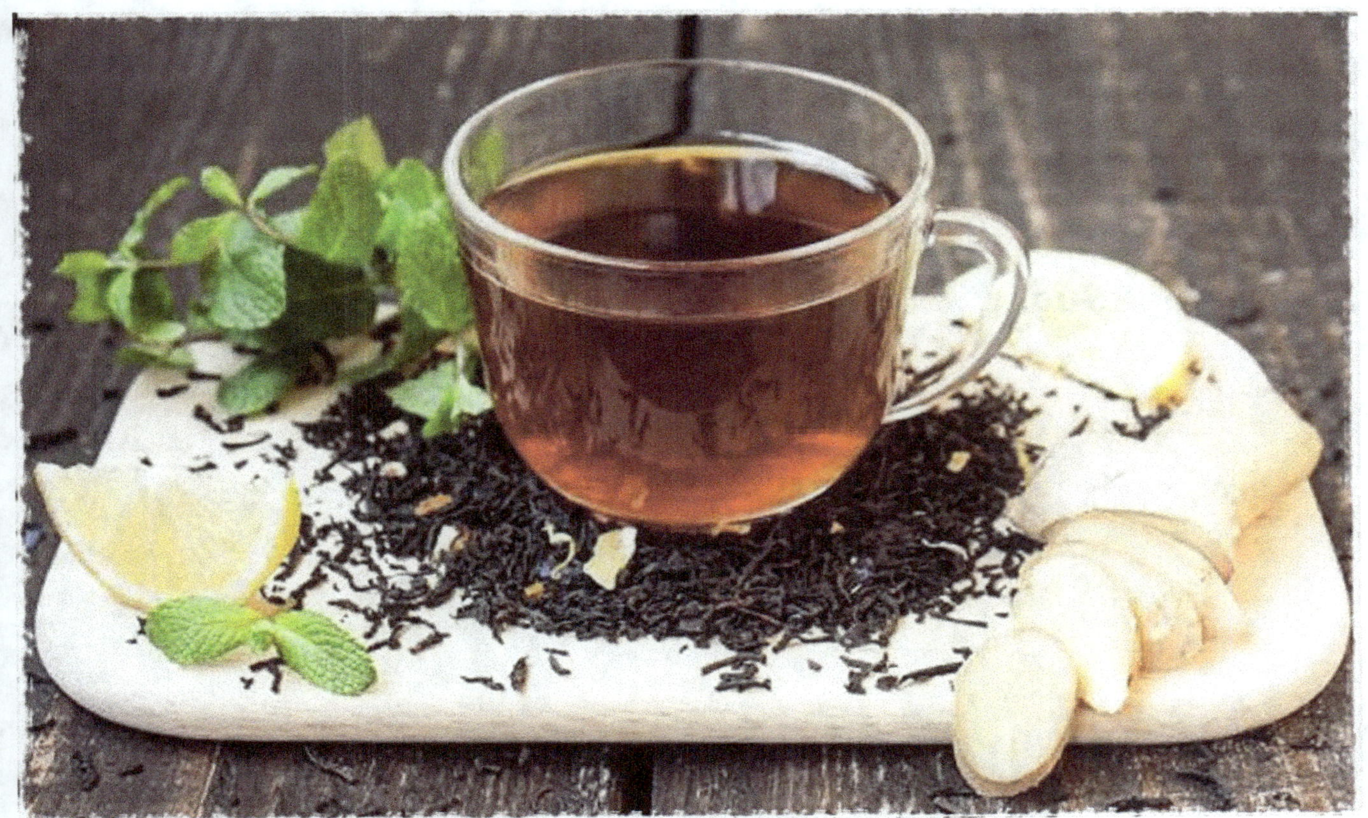

Preparation Time: 3 minutes
Cooking Time: 3 minutes
Servings: 1

Ingredients:

- 1 cup water
- ½ inch ginger
- 1 teaspoon tea leaves
- ½ lemon
- ½ teaspoon honey

Preparation:

1. Boil water and add ginger and tea leaves in it.
2. Cover the lid and cook for about 3 minutes.
3. Open the lid and squeeze lemon in it.
4. Take out and add honey.

5. Serve and enjoy!

Serving Suggestions: Serve with lemon on the top.

Variation Tip: Use brown sugar instead of honey.

Nutritional Information per Serving:

Calories: 22| **Fat:** 0.1g| **Sat Fat:** 0g| **Carbohydrates:** 6.2g|

Fiber: 0.9g| **Sugar:** 3.6g| **Protein:** 0.4g

Twyla Sands Ginger Tea

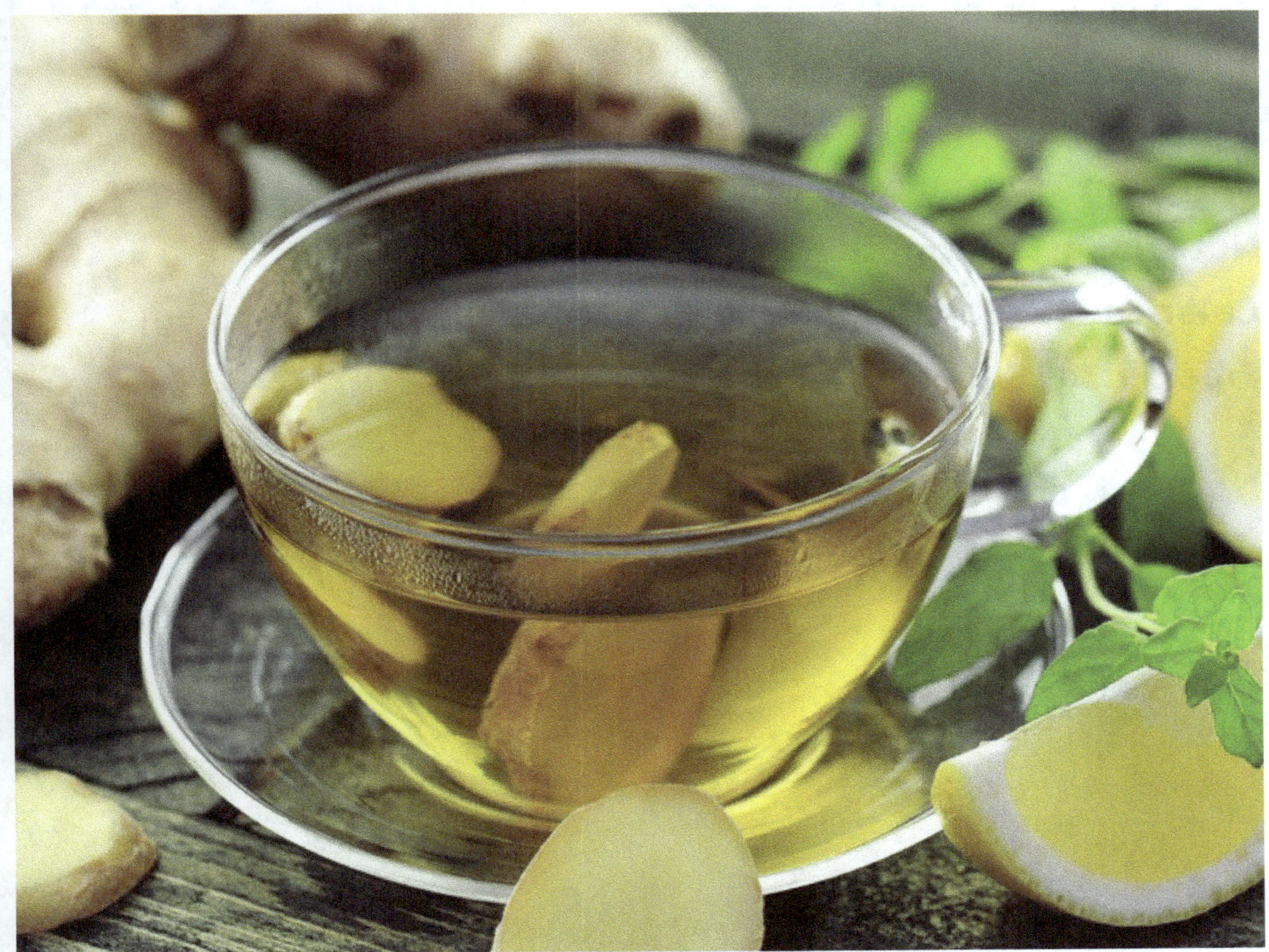

Preparation Time: 2 minutes
Cooking Time: 9 minutes
Servings: 2

Ingredients:

- 2 inch ginger, sliced
- 2 cinnamon sticks
- 2 cups water
- 1 lemon

Preparation:

1. Add water, cinnamon sticks, and ginger in a saucepan.

2. Boil it for 5 minutes and take out.
3. Squeeze lemon in tea and serve.

Serving Suggestions: Before serving, garnish with cinnamon powder.

Variation Tip: You can also use mint leaves to enhance taste.

Nutritional Information per Serving:

Calories: 20| **Fat:** 0.2g| **Sat Fat:** 0.1g| **Carbohydrates:** 5.8g|

Fiber: 2.3g| **Sugar:** 0.8g| **Protein:** 0.6g

Robert Currie Lavender Mint Tea

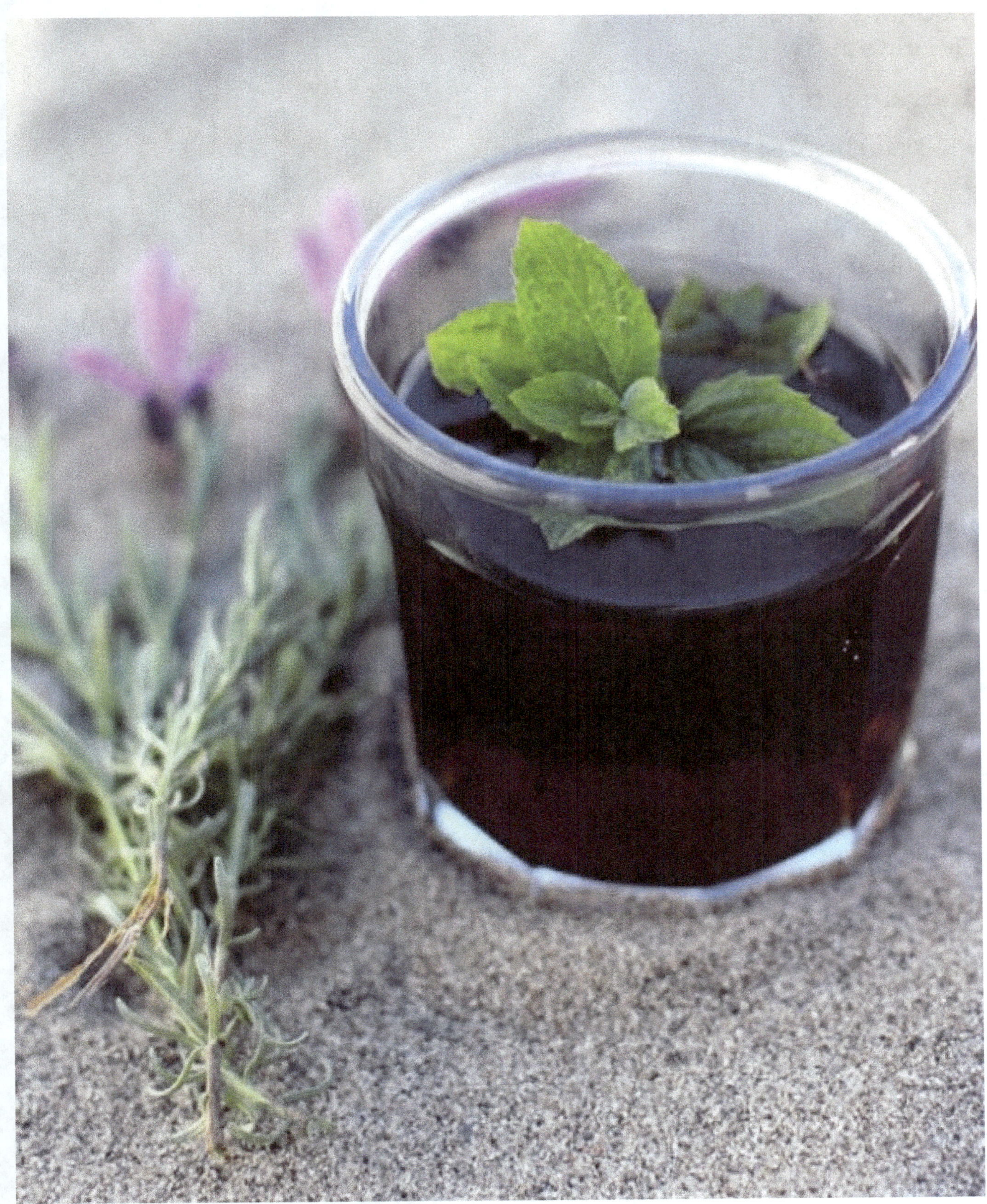

Preparation Time: 2 minutes
Cooking Time: 12 minutes
Servings: 2

Ingredients:

- 3 cups water
- ½ cup fresh mint leaves
- ¼ cup fresh lavender petals

Preparation:

1. Add lavender petals and mint leaves in water and bring to boil.
2. Simmer for about 10 minutes and strain out mint leaves and lavender petals.
3. Serve hot and enjoy!

Serving Suggestions: Squeeze lemon before serving.

Variation Tip: You can also use cardamom for an even better taste.

Nutritional Information per Serving:

Calories: 20| **Fat:** 0.4g| **Sat Fat:** 0g| **Carbohydrates:** 3.5g| **Fiber:** 1.6g| **Sugar:** 0g| **Protein:** 1.3g

Veronica Lee Chamomile Tea

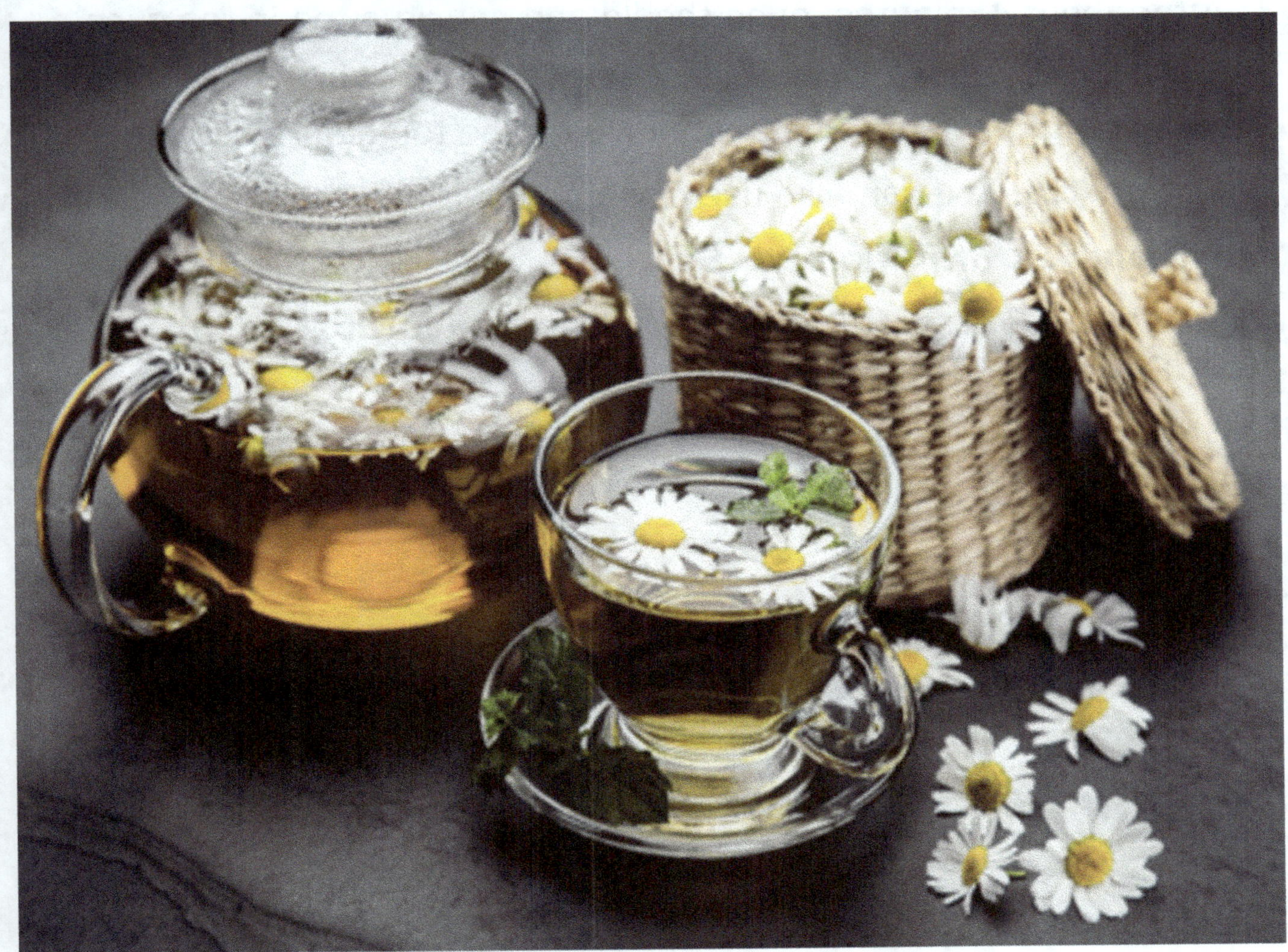

Preparation Time: 2 minutes
Cooking Time: 5 minutes

Servings: 1

Ingredients:

- 1 cup water
- ½ teaspoon honey
- 1½ teaspoon dried chamomile
- 2 cardamoms

Preparation:

1. In a saucepan, add water, cardamoms, and dried chamomile.

2. Bring the mixture to boil and close the lid.
3. After about 4 minutes, open the lid and pour the tea in tea cups.
4. Add in honey and serve hot.

Serving Suggestions: Put chamomile on the top before serving.

Variation Tip: You can also use cinnamon sticks in the tea.

Nutritional Information per Serving:

Calories: 23| **Fat:** 0.3g| **Sat Fat:** 0g| **Carbohydrates:** 5.6g| **Fiber:** 1.1g| **Sugar:** 2.9g| **Protein:** 0.4g

Theodore Mullens Apple Cinnamon Tea

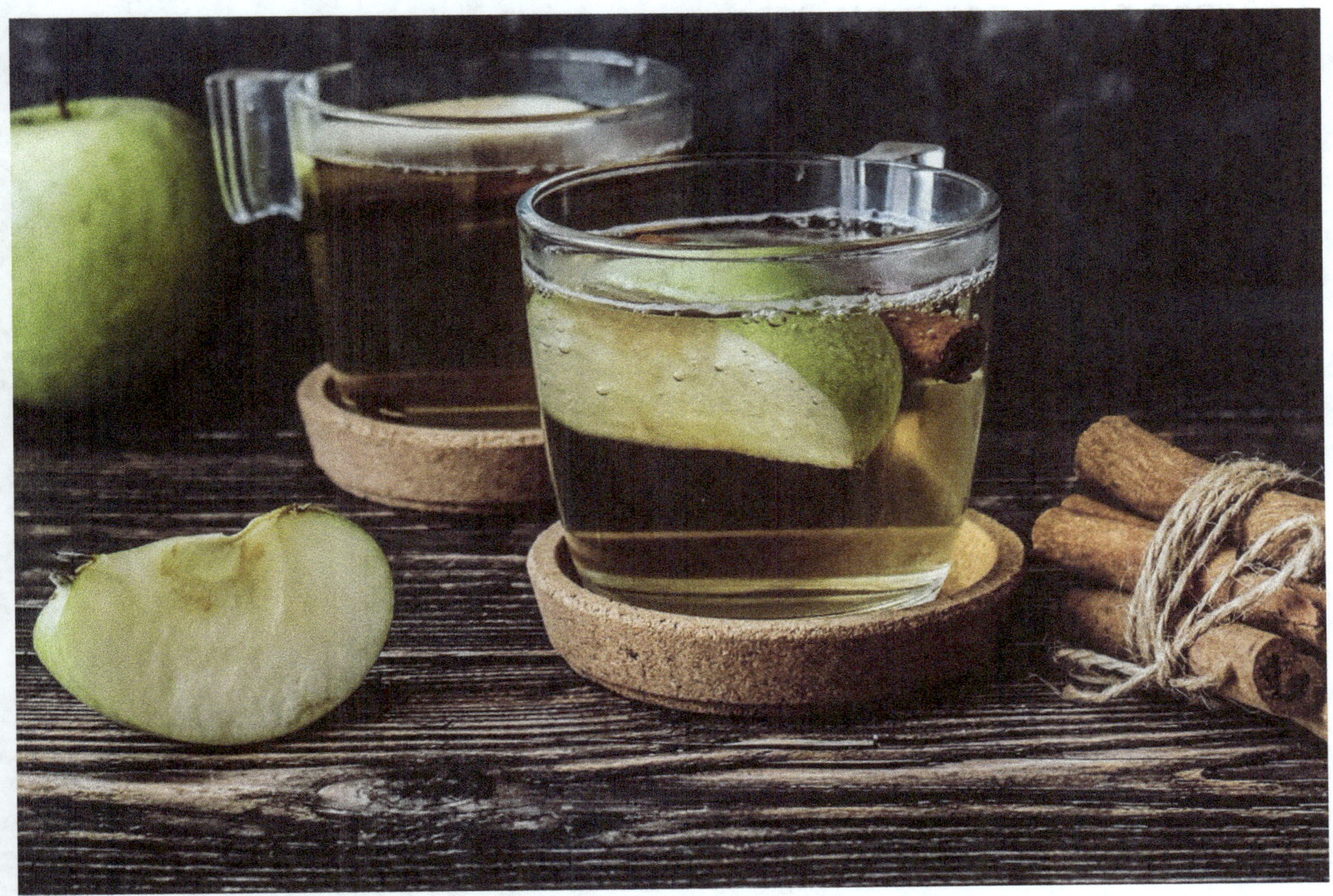

Preparation Time: 3 minutes
Cooking Time: 20 minutes
Servings: 4

Ingredients:

- 1½ apples, sliced
- 2 cinnamon stick
- 6 cups water
- ½ teaspoon chopped cardamom
- ½ teaspoon honey

Preparation:

1. Add apple slices, cinnamon sticks and cardamom in boiling water and simmer for about 15 minutes.

2. Open the lid and pour the tea in tea cups.
3. Add in honey and serve hot.

Serving Suggestions: Add in apple slices and cinnamon sticks in tea cups before serving.

Variation Tip: You can use sugar instead of honey.

Nutritional Information per Serving:

Calories: 166| **Fat:** 0.6g| **Sat Fat:** 0g| **Carbohydrates:** 44.2g|

Fiber: 8.1g| **Sugar:** 32.6g| **Protein:** 0.9g

Patrick Brewer Milk Tea

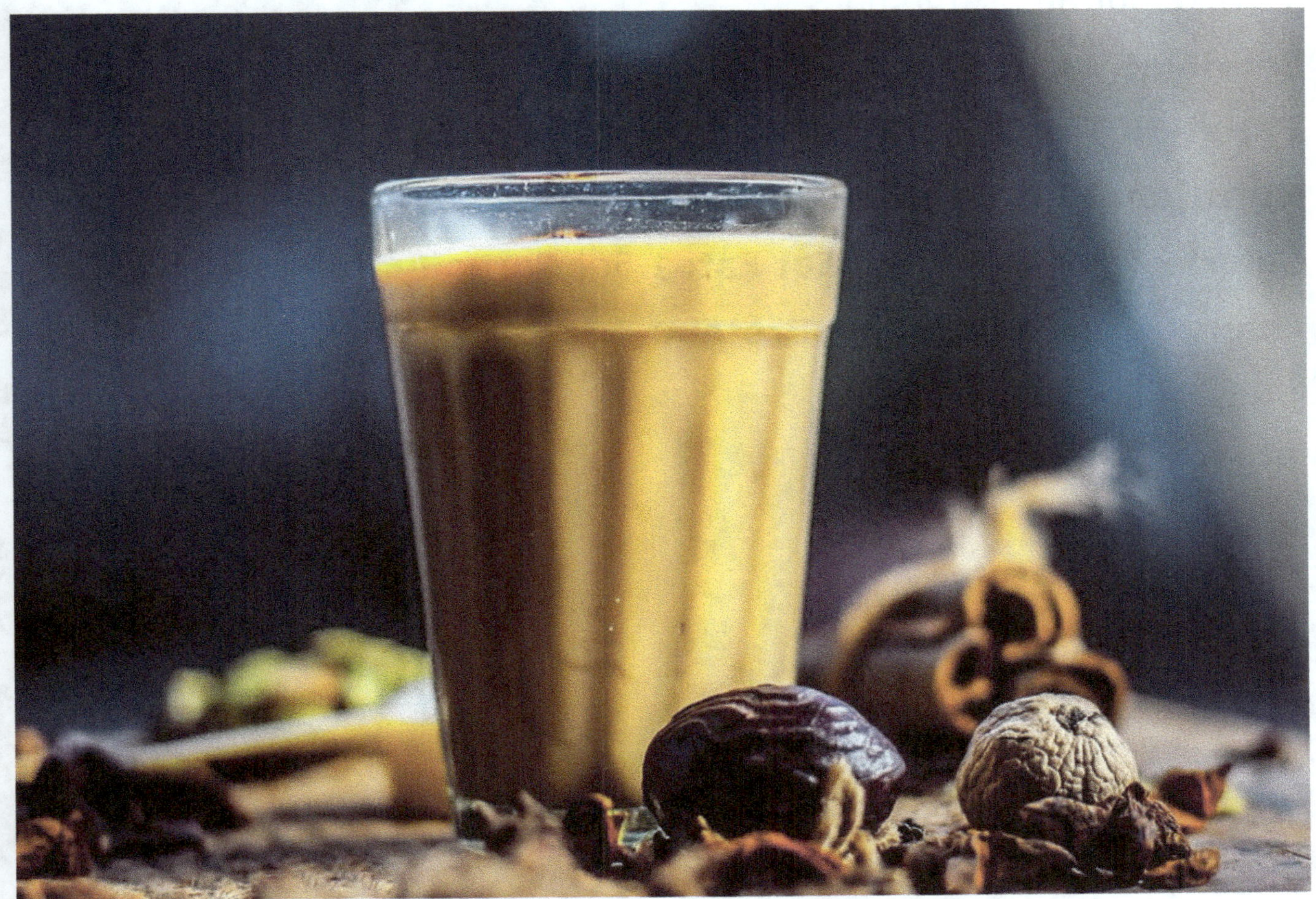

Preparation Time: 4 minutes
Cooking Time: 10 minutes

Servings: 4

Ingredients:

- 2 cups milk
- 1 cup water
- 4 teaspoons tea powder
- 4 teaspoons sugar

Preparation:

1. Add water, tea powder and sugar in a pan.
2. Boil for about 4 minutes and add in milk.

3. Cover the lid and simmer for about 6 to 7 minutes.
4. Take out and serve hot.

Serving Suggestions: Top with cinnamon powder before serving.

Variation Tip: You can add cardamom to enhance taste.

Nutritional Information per Serving:

Calories: 78| **Fat:** 2.5g| **Sat Fat:** 1.5g| **Carbohydrates:** 10.4g|

Fiber: 0.1g| **Sugar:** 9.5g| **Protein:** 4.1g

Johnny Rose Green Tea

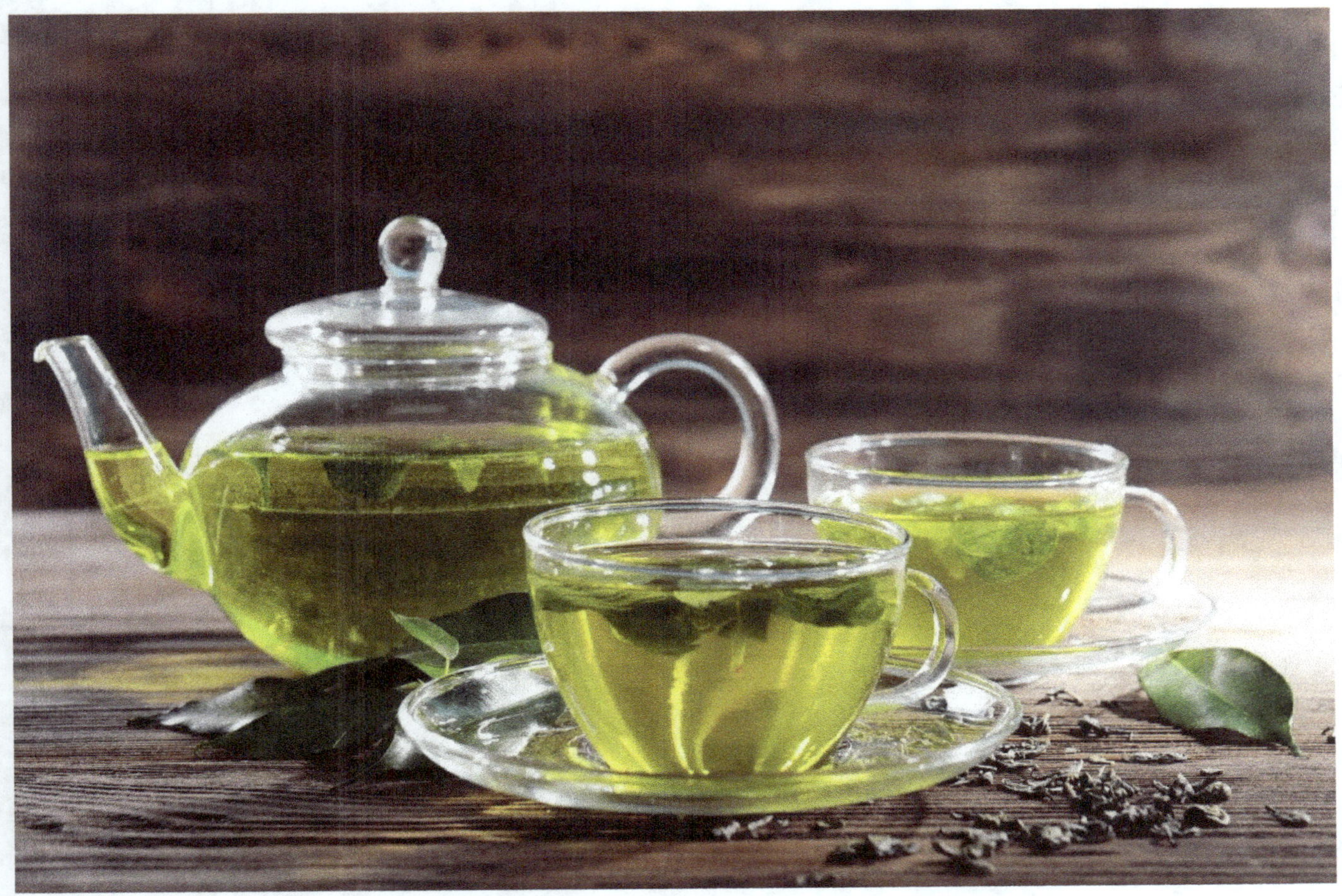

Preparation Time: 4 minutes
Cooking Time: 5 minutes
Servings: 4

Ingredients:

- 4 cups water
- 4 teaspoons green tea leaves
- 2 tablespoons honey

Preparation:

1. Add water in a saucepan and put it over medium-high heat.
2. Turn off the heat and add in green tea leaves.
3. Close the lid and keep the mixture covered for about 3 minutes.
4. Take out and top with mint leaves.

5. Serve hot and enjoy!

Serving Suggestions: Squeeze lemon in green tea before serving.

Variation Tip: Honey can be omitted.

Nutritional Information per Serving:

Calories: 34| **Fat:** 0g| **Sat Fat:** 0g| **Carbohydrates:** 9.2g| **Fiber:** 0g| **Sugar:** 8.6g| **Protein:** 0g

Conclusion

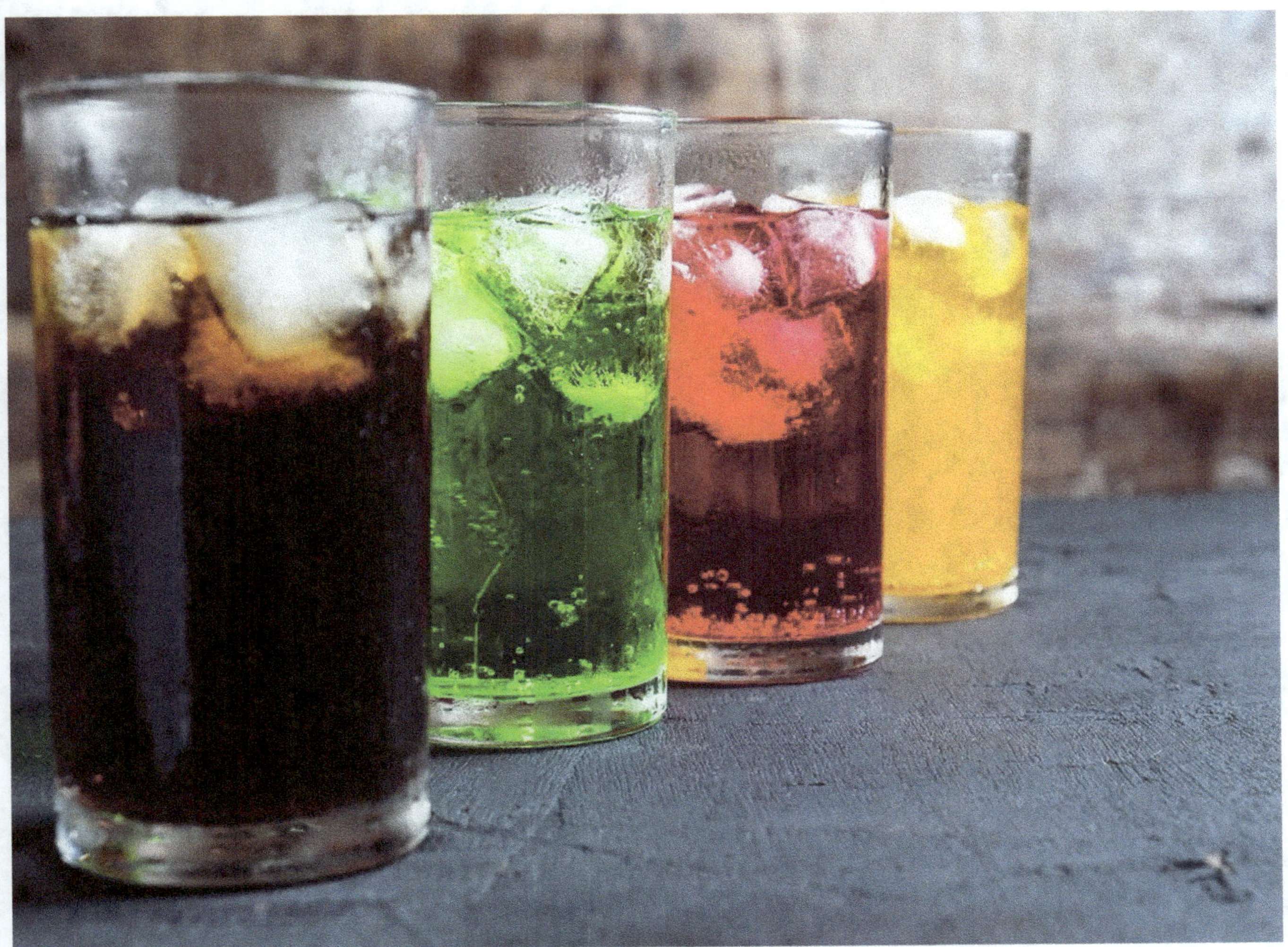

The Unofficial Schitt's Creek Drink Cookbook is solely inspired by the famous humour TV show, i.e., Schitt's Creek. The book is based on the idea of blending food and humour together to provide you with instant relief from the never-ending worries of life. The cookbook provides you with various beverages and drinks that are genuinely inspired by prominent places and characters of the TV show. The recipes are well-scripted, and all the necessary instructions are thoroughly written to provide you with the utmost convenience.